101 wire EARRINGS

Step-by-Step Projects & Techniques

DENISE PECK

Editor of *Step by Step Wire Jewelry*

INTERWEAVE.

interweavestore.com

TECH EDITOR
Jamie Hogsett

PHOTOGRAPHY
Joe Coca

DESIGN
Liz Quan

PRODUCTION
Katherine Jackson

Interweave Press LLC
201 East Fourth Street
Loveland, CO 80537
Interweavestore.com

Printed in China by Asia Pacific Offset.

Library of Congress Cataloging-in-Publication Data

Peck, Denise.
 101 wire earrings : step-by-step techniques and projects / Denise Peck.
    p. cm.
 Includes bibliographical references and index.
 ISBN 978-1-59668-141-5 (pbk.)
 1. Jewelry making. 2. Wire craft. 3. Earrings. I. Title.
    II. Title: One hundred one wire earrings.
 TT212.P4245 2009
 739.27—dc22
                            2009008794

10 9 8 7 6 5 4 3 2 1

DEDICATION

For my mother, who told me, when I was a teenager, that I should learn to make jewelry. And who, at ninety-one, is still as excited about going to a bead show as I am.

– Denise Peck

TABLE OF CONTENTS

Projects

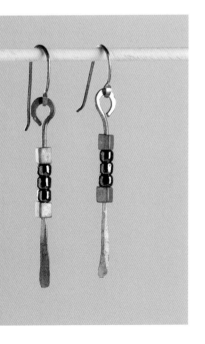

INTRODUCTION

Chances are, if you're a jewelry lover, you frequently find yourself browsing jewelry departments and marveling at all the beautiful earrings. And probably on more than one occasion you've whispered to yourself, "I could make that." Well, you're right! Almost all pierced earrings are made of only two design elements: a dangle, or stationary decoration, and an ear wire, or post. And they all use wire. Once you know a few basic rules about working with wire and the elementary steps for making the key pieces, the sky's the limit! Have you heard—you can never have too many earrings!

Whether you're already a jewelry maker or you're just venturing into the world of beads and wire, you'll find earring designs here that will tickle your creativity. With the resources given for each project, you can follow along step by step, or you can throw in some of your own beads or found objects and make them your very own. As a bonus, many of the designs featured include an easy suggestion for another option for a quick change-up to the look.

You probably already own some of the basic tools required: a chain-nose pliers, which are just like needle-nose pliers, but without teeth; a ball-peen hammer; a wire cutter. Most of the designs in this book can be made with three or four simple tools. There's a comprehensive glossary of tools—those you definitely need, and some you may want to add to your toolbox.

Because almost every pair of earrings uses ear wires, I've included a special Techniques section (pages 14–23) of clearly photographed instructions for making several different ear wire designs, along with matching head pins. This section also outlines the rest of the simple wireworking processes you need to make all 101 designs.

The projects are conveniently labeled by skill level. If you master the simple ones, you can easily work your way through to the more challenging designs. Or, you can flip through all the projects, mark your favorites and dive right in. Either way, everything you need to learn how to make just about any pair of earrings is right here. So take another shopping trip and know that, *yes,* you can definitely make that pair of earrings!

WIRE PRIMER

One of the best things about working with wire is that it's such a forgiving medium. If you make a mistake, you can often restraighten the wire and begin again. Additionally, you can buy practice wire very inexpensively and create with impunity! Copper, brass, and colored craft wire are available in hardware and craft stores, and all of them can produce finished pieces every bit as beautiful as sterling silver and gold.

Wire comes in a large variety of metals, shapes, and sizes. The size or diameter of wire is known as the gauge. In the United States, the standard is Brown & Sharpe, also known as American Wire Gauge (AWG). The diameter of wire in inches or millimeters is translated into a numeral from 0 to 34, the higher the number, the thinner the wire. Most of the projects in this book use wire in 14 gauge through 24 gauge.

Wire also comes in a variety of shapes. You can buy round, half-round, and square wire. Round is most commonly used and easily available—all projects in this book call for round wire unless otherwise instructed. Half-round has a flat side and is commonly used for ring shanks, and square wire has four flat sides. Both half-round and square wire must be ordered from a jeweler's supplier. In most cases, the choice of shape is purely aesthetic.

Additionally, a jeweler's supplier will offer wire in three hardnesses: dead-soft, half-hard, and full-hard. Dead soft wire is best if you're going to be manipulating it a lot because wire work-hardens as you work with it. Work-hardening stiffens the wire and makes it harder to bend. Eventually it can become so brittle that it can break with additional manipulation.

If you're weaving, coiling, or spiraling, you should work with dead-soft wire, as it's much easier on the hands. If you're making ear wires or not planning on working the wire too

gauge	round	half-round	square
2g	●	◗	■
3g	●	◗	■
4g	●	◗	■
6g	●	◗	■
7g	●	◗	■
8g	●	◗	■
9g	●	◗	■
10g	●	◗	■
11g	●	◗	■
12g	●	◗	■
13g	●	◗	■
14g	●	◗	■
16g	●	◗	■
18g	•	◗	▪
19g	•	◗	▪
20g	•	◗	▪
21g	•	◗	▪
22g	•	◗	▪
24g	•	◗	▪
26g	•	◗	▪

much, you can start with half-hard wire, which is already stiffer than dead-soft wire. There are no projects in this book that call for full-hard wire.

You can make jewelry out of both base-metal wire and precious-metal wire. The most common base-metal wire used in jewelry is copper, though aluminum, nickel silver, and brass are also available.

Sterling silver and gold wire are precious metals. The cost of gold wire is often prohibitive, so a common alternative is gold-filled wire, which is base-metal wire covered with an outer layer of gold. Gold-filled wire is preferable to gold-plated wire because gold plating scratches and wears off easily.

As with the shape of the wire, the choice of metal is usually just a matter of personal preference.

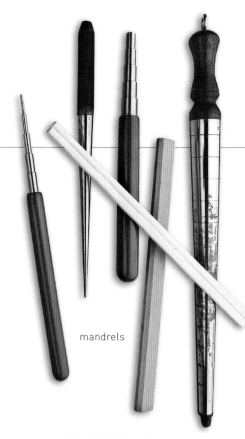

mandrels

TOOLS

Many of the earring designs in this book require five simple tools; a set of pliers, wire cutters, a ring mandrel, a large stepped mandrel and a coiling tool. As you become more adept at jewelry making, you may want to expand your toolbox to include some of the tools below. Tool prices reflect the quality of the tools you're buying, and range from very inexpensive to very expensive. A good set of pliers will be the best investment you can make.

GENERAL
General tools range from basic necessities like flush cutters to mandrels for forming and gauges for measuring.

flush cutters
These are also called side cutters because the cut is made to the side. They have pointed, angled jaws that allow very close cuts in tight places. One side of the jaws is almost flat, the other is concave. Always hold the flat side of the cutters against your work and the concave side against the waste. The flat side creates a nice flush end on your work. Flush cutters are sold with a maximum gauge-cutting capacity; be sure to use cutters that can accommodate the wire you're using.

wire gauge
Also known as the Brown & Sharpe wire gauge, this tool looks a bit like a flat round gear. It measures the diameter of your wire and is an essential tool for wire jewelry making (see page 8).

mandrels
A spindle, rod, or bar around which you can bend metal or wire. They come in a variety of shapes and sizes. Some are made specifically for bracelets, rings, and making bezels. Almost anything can be used as a mandrel to shape wire, including wooden dowels and other pieces of wire. A Sharpie is the perfect shape for making French ear wires.

coiling gizmo™
When making a lot of small coils, this tool makes it a snap to coil many inches in a few minutes. Use a small c-clamp to anchor it to your table. It comes with two different size coiling mandrels for small and larger diameter coils.

butane torch
Small handheld torches are available in hardware stores and jewelry suppliers. They use butane and are filled from a canister like you would fill a cigarette lighter. Use these torches to make balled head pins and ear wires, which can be expensive to buy pre-made.

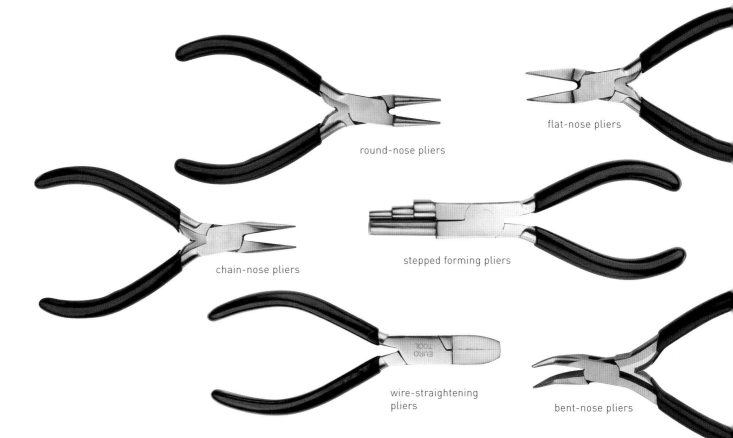

round-nose pliers

flat-nose pliers

chain-nose pliers

stepped forming pliers

wire-straightening pliers

bent-nose pliers

PLIERS
There are many varieties of pliers on the market. These six basics are all you need to make all the earrings in this book.

chain-nose pliers
The workhorse of wire tools, chain-nose pliers are like needle-nose pliers but without teeth that can mar your wire. They are used for grasping wire, opening and closing jump rings, and making sharp angled bends. It's a good idea to have at least two pairs in your workshop.

round-nose pliers
Another wireworker's necessity, round-nose pliers have pointed, graduated round jaws. They are used for making jump rings, simple loops, and curved bends in wire.

stepped forming pliers
Forming pliers come in different sizes and shapes. Stepped forming pliers have one chain-nose, concave jaw and one jaw of various-sized-round barrels. They're perfect for wrapping loops of consistent size.

wire-straightening pliers
These are also called nylon-jaw pliers because the jaws are made of hard nylon. Pulling wire through the clamped jaws will straighten any bends or kinks. They can also be used to hold, bend, or shape wire without marring the metal. Keep in mind that every time you pull wire through straightening pliers, you're work-hardening it more, making it more brittle and harder to manipulate.

flat-nose pliers
Flat-nose pliers have broad flat jaws and are good for making sharp bends in wire, grasping spirals, and holding components.

bent-nose pliers
Also called bent chain-nose pliers, these are similar to chain-nose pliers but have a bent tip allowing access to tight places for tasks such as tightening coils and tucking in ends. Use two pairs together to open and close jump rings.

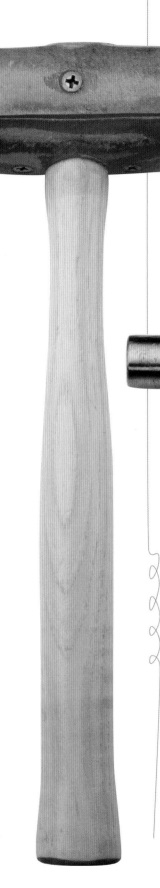

HAMMERING TOOLS are used to flatten wire, add texture, and work-harden. Supplemental tools such as an awl, used with a hammer, can pierce holes in wire.

rawhide mallet

A hammer made of rawhide, this can be used on metal and wire without marring it. It's good for tapping wire into place or for hardening wire.

ball-peen hammer

Another staple in the studio, this hammer has one round domed head and one round flat head. The round head is used for making little dents for texture, while the flat head is used for flattening wire.

awl

This common household tool comes in handy in a wire studio. A very sharp pointed tool, an awl often has a wooden or acrylic ball for a handle. Use it with a hammer to punch holes in flattened wire.

steel bench block

A bench block provides a small and portable hard surface on which to hammer wire. It's made of polished steel and is usually only ¾" (1.9 cm) thick and a few inches square. Use a bench block with a ball-peen hammer for flattening or texturing wire.

FINISHING TOOLS are used to smooth sharp wire ends, alter the wire color, and buff your earrings to the perfect shine.

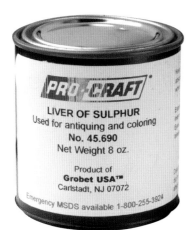

liver of sulfur

Liver of sulfur is a chemical traditionally used to darken silver wire. It comes in a liquid or solid chunk form and is used for oxidizing, or antiquing, wire. When a small amount is mixed with hot water, it will turn a piece of wire dipped in it from blue to gray to black. Very fine steel wool can be used to finish oxidized silver.

wire smoother

This little tool has what's called a cup bur on the end of it. A cup bur is a tiny cup-shaped file. When you twirl the end of an ear wire inside the cup bur, it smooths and files away all the sharp edges.

polishing cloth

Jewelry polishing cloths are infused with a polishing compound and can be used for cleaning wire, eliminating tarnish, and hardening wire—pulling wire through the cloth repeatedly will stiffen, or work-harden, it. Pro Polish pads are one of the most popular brands.

needle files

Needle files are made for smoothing sharp ends of metal and wire. They're small and fine and come in different shapes for different purposes. A flat needle file is often all you need for smoothing wire ends.

TECHNIQUES

As with tools, there a few essential wire techniques for making most earrings. Almost all the earrings in this book require some sort of head pin (the wire on which you thread your beads) and an ear wire (the hook that goes through your ear). Once you've mastered making these elements, you can add to your repertoire as the designs require.

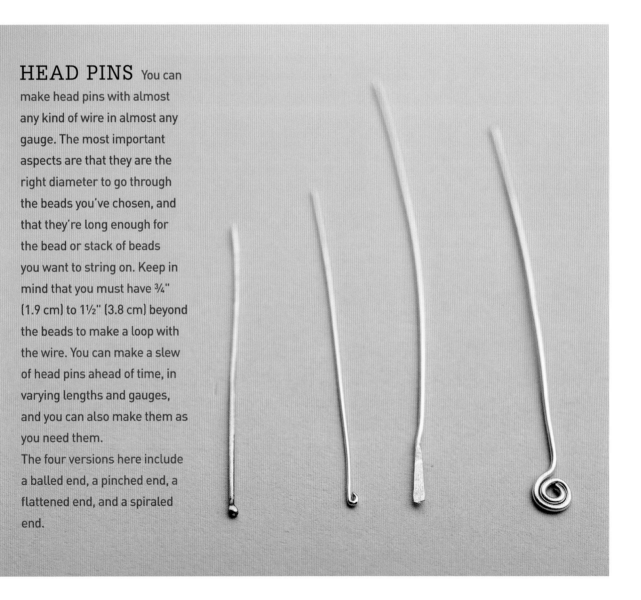

HEAD PINS You can make head pins with almost any kind of wire in almost any gauge. The most important aspects are that they are the right diameter to go through the beads you've chosen, and that they're long enough for the bead or stack of beads you want to string on. Keep in mind that you must have ¾" (1.9 cm) to 1½" (3.8 cm) beyond the beads to make a loop with the wire. You can make a slew of head pins ahead of time, in varying lengths and gauges, and you can also make them as you need them.

The four versions here include a balled end, a pinched end, a flattened end, and a spiraled end.

spiraled head pin

Using any wire, make a tiny loop at the end of the wire with the smallest end of round-nose pliers (figure 1). With chain- or flat-nose pliers, hold the loop you just made flat in the jaws and use the thumb of your other hand to push the long wire around the loop to form a spiral (figure 2). When the spiral is the size you want, use your chain- or flat-nose pliers to bend the remaining wire out from the spiral at a 90° angle (figure 3).

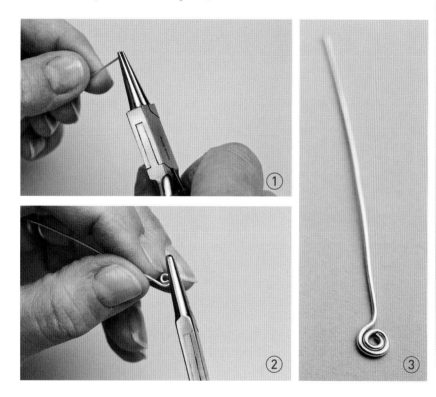

pinched head pin

This is the quickest and easiest head pin to make. Using any wire, bend one end up 1/16" (0.2 cm) and pinch it snugly against the length of the wire.

balled head pin

Using copper, sterling, or fine silver wire, hold one end of your wire with a pliers or tweezers and hold the other end perpendicular in the blue, hottest portion of the flame on your butane torch (below). When the wire balls up to the size you desire, remove it from the flame and quench it in a bowl of cool water. Copper and sterling will require that you remove the oxidation caused by the flame with a little steel wool.

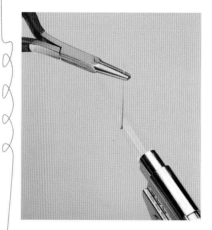

flattened head pin

Using any wire, hold one end of the wire against your steel bench block and hammer 1/8" (0.3 cm) flat with a ball-peen hammer (right).

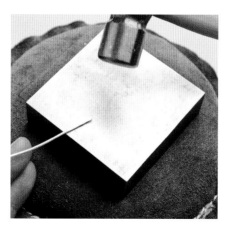

EAR WIRES

Making ear wires is one of the simplest techniques with the greatest benefits. First, it saves you from having to buy them, and they can be costly. Second, it allows you to personalize your earrings right down to the ear wires, in whatever design you want. Every head pin you just learned to make can be made into a custom ear wire!

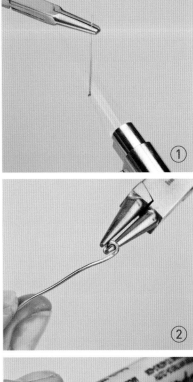

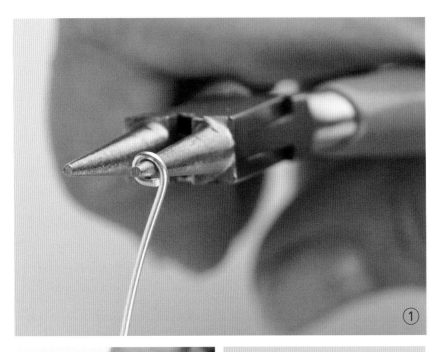

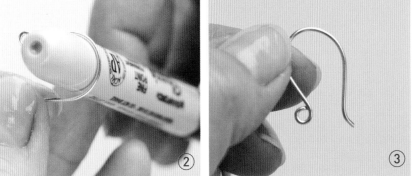

basic ear wires

Make a small loop on the end of 1½" (3.8 cm) of wire **(figure 1)**. Hold the loop against a Sharpie marker and bend the wire over the marker away from the loop **(figure 2)**. Use round-nose pliers to make a small bend outward at the end of the wire **(figure 3)**.

balled ear wires

Ball up the end of 1¾" (4.4 cm) of sterling, copper, or fine silver wire and quench in water to cool **(figure 1)**. Use round-nose pliers to make a small loop at the balled end **(figure 2)**. Hold the loop against a Sharpie marker and bend the wire over the marker away from the loop **(figure 3)**.

flattened ear wires

Hammer flat the tip of 1¾" (4.4 cm) of wire (figure 1). Use round-nose pliers to bend up the flattened tip (figure 2). Hold the loop against a Sharpie marker and bend the wire over the marker away from the loop (figure 3).

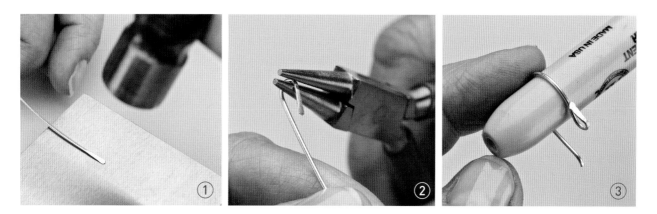

spiraled ear wires

Create a spiral at the end of 1¾" (4.4 cm) of wire (figure 1). Hold the spiral flat in your chain-nose pliers and bend the wire perpendicular to the spiral (figure 2). Hold the spiral against a Sharpie marker and bend the wire over the marker away from the spiral (figure 3). Pinch the spiral against the finished ear wire (figure 4).

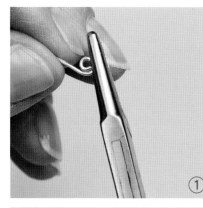
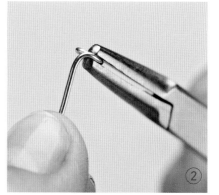

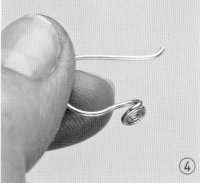

LOOPS are secure connections between ear wires and other elements of the earrings.

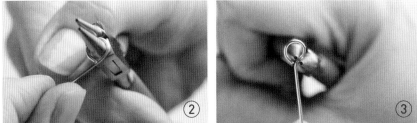

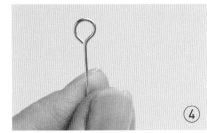

simple loop

Grasp the end of the wire in round-nose pliers so you can just see the tip of the wire (figure 1). Rotate the pliers fully until you've made a complete loop (figure 2). Remove the pliers. Reinsert the tip of the pliers to grasp the wire directly across from the opening of the loop. Make a sharp 45° bend across from the opening (figure 3), centering the loop over the length of the wire like a lollipop (figure 4).

wrapped loop

Grasp the wire about 2" (5.1 cm) from the end with chain-nose pliers. Use your fingers to bend the wire flat against the pliers to 90° (figure 1). Use round-nose pliers to grasp the wire right at the bend you just made, holding the pliers perpendicular to the tabletop. Pull the wire up and over the top of the round-nose pliers (figure 2). Pull the pliers out and put the lower jaw back into the loop you just made (figure 3). Continue pulling the wire around the bottom jaw of the pliers into a full round loop (figure 4). With your fingers or chain-nose pliers, wrap the wire around the neck of the lower wire two or three times (figures 5–6).

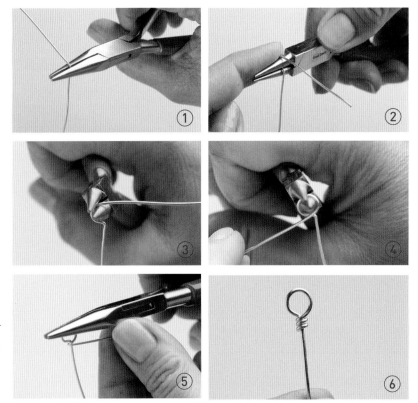

briolette loop

For top-drilled stones, insert a wire through the hole and bend up both sides so that they cross over the top of the stone (figure 1). (You will only need a short length on one side.) Make a bend in each of the wires so they point straight up off the top of the stone. Use flush cutters to trim the short wire so that it's no longer than ⅛" (0.3 cm) (figure 2). Pinch the two wires together with chain-nose pliers and bend the longer wire over the top of the shorter wire to 90° (figure 3). Make a wrapped loop by switching to round-nose pliers and pulling the long wire up and over the round jaw (figures 4–5). Wrap the neck of the two wires together two or three times to secure (figures 6–7).

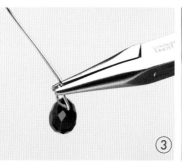

COILS + SPIRALS are great decorative additions to wire earrings. String a coil of wire onto a straight wire for an extra bit of detail on a project. Spirals can be added to head pins, ear wires, dangles, and more.

coiling

Coils can be made on any round mandrel, including another piece of wire. Hold one end of the wire tightly against the mandrel with your thumb and coil the length up the mandrel. Be sure to wrap snugly and keep the coils right next to one another **(figure 1)**. Flush cut both ends **(figure 2)**.

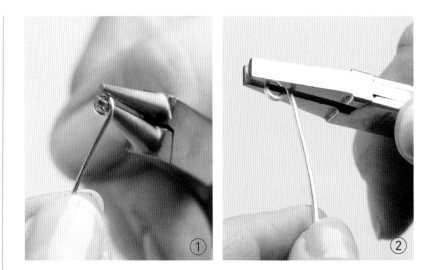

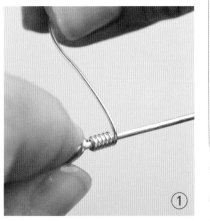

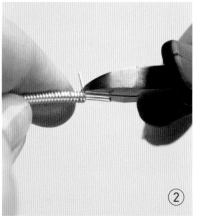

spiraling

Make a very small loop with round-nose pliers **(figure 1)**. Grasp the loop in flat-nose pliers and use the thumb of your other hand to push the wire around the loop **(figure 2)**. Continue to move the spiral around in the jaws of the flat-nose pliers to enable you to enlarge the coil **(figure 3)**.

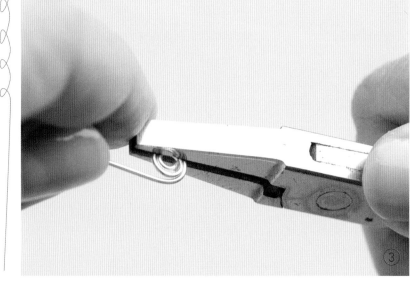

JUMP RINGS are used to connect components or as design elements, especially when made with colorful craft wire.

making jump rings

Coil wire snugly around a mandrel (figure 1). Each single coil will make one jump ring. Remove the mandrel. Use flush cutters to cut through all the rings at the same spot along the length of the coil, snipping one or two at a time (figure 2). They will fall away and each ring will be slightly open (figure 3). The jump rings you make will have the inner diameter (ID) of the mandrel you used to make them.

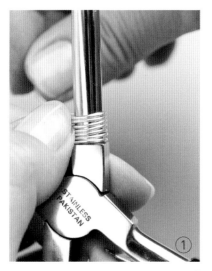

TIP When purchasing jump rings, note that some vendors sell them by inner diameter measurements and some vendors sell them by outer diameter measurements. The difference is minuscule and only essential if you're working on a complex chain mail design.

opening and closing jump rings

Always use two chain- or bent-nose pliers to open and close jump rings. Grasp the ring on each side of the opening with pliers (figure 1). Gently push one side away from you while pulling the other side toward you, so the ring opens from side to side (figure 2). To close, reverse the directions of your hands.

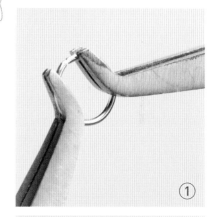

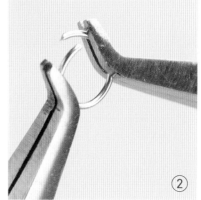

PIERCING + OXIDIZING are fun ways to add
additional detail to your earring designs. Small pierced holes turn a piece of wire
into a link, a dangle, and more. Oxidizing adds color and dimension to wire.

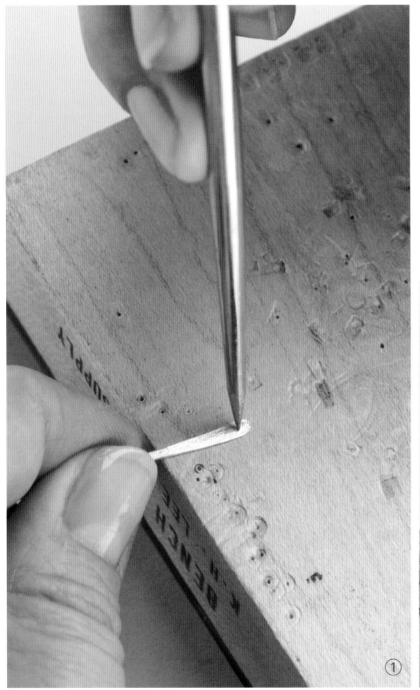

piercing

If wire has been flattened, you can pierce it with an awl to make a hole for connecting other elements, such as ear wires. It's best to work on a scrap piece of wood. Take a sharp awl and position it where you want the hole. Push firmly to make an impression—a starter spot **(figure 1)**. Then place the point of the awl in the impression and strike the top sharply with a hammer **(figure 2)**.

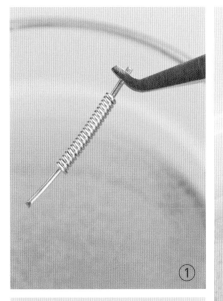

(1)

(2)

oxidizing

Liver of sulfur is used to darken, or patina, wire. Dissolve a small lump of liver of sulfur in very hot water. Dip your piece into the solution **(figure 1)**. Depending on the temperature of the solution, and the length of time you leave the piece in it, the wire can turn a variety of colors, including gold, blue, and black **(figure 2)**. Remove the piece when it reaches the desired color **(figure 3)**. Dry and polish it lightly to remove some of the patina **(figure 4)** but leave the dark color in the recesses of the piece **(figure 5)**.

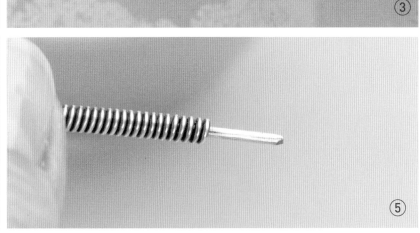

(3)

(4)

(5)

PROJECTS

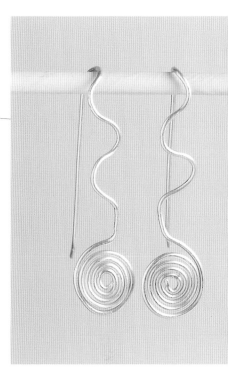

If you can do the techniques outlined in this book, you can make all of these earrings!

On each pair of earrings, you'll see one of the three symbols below. These symbols represent the approximate time each pair will take to make. If you need a quick gift or want to practice the techniques you've just learned, go for something in Level 1. If you have more time on your hands or want more of a challenge, try a pair from Level 2 or 3.

◎ **LEVEL 1:** 5 to 10 minutes

◎◎ **LEVEL 2:** 10 to 20 minutes

◎◎◎ **LEVEL 3:** 20 to 30 minutes

RANDOMLY
RIPPLED

MATERIALS
16" (40.6 cm) of sterling silver dead-soft 18-gauge wire

2 blue 20mm lampworked glass discs

1 pair sterling silver ear wires

TOOLS
Flush cutters

⅛" (0.3 cm) steel mandrel

Round-nose pliers

FINISHED SIZE
2½" (6.4 cm)

1. Cut the wire in half.

2. Use 1 wire to string 1 disc to the center of the wire. Bend the wire in half, letting the bead sit in the bend.

3. Hold the disc and wire against the mandrel. Randomly wrap both ends of the wire around the mandrel, crisscrossing and overlapping the wire as you go, until you've completely wrapped one end of the wire and have about ½" (1.3 cm) of wire remaining on the other end. Slide the piece off the mandrel. Use round-nose pliers to tuck in the wrapped-wire end.

4. Use round-nose pliers to form a simple loop with the remaining wire.

5. Attach 1 ear wire to the simple loop.

6. Repeat Steps 2 to 5 for the second earring.

7. Hang the pair side by side and, if necessary, adjust to the same length by pinching the random coils together or pulling them apart.

RESOURCE: Lampworked glass discs: Kab's Creative Concepts.

Designer Kerry Bogert

GREEN BERETS

◎

MATERIALS

4½" (11.4 cm) of sterling silver 16-gauge dead-soft wire

2 olive green size 6° seed beads

2 blue-green 12mm clay beads

2 purple and blue-green 18mm lampworked glass discs

1 pair sterling silver ear wires

TOOLS

Flush cutters

Round-nose pliers

Ball-peen hammer

Bench block

FINISHED SIZE

2¼" (5.7 cm)

1. Cut the wire in half.

2. Use the hammer to splay flat one end of 1 wire.

3. String 1 seed bead, 1 clay bead, and 1 lampworked glass disc. Form a simple loop.

4. Attach an ear wire to the simple loop.

5. Repeat Steps 2 to 4 for the second earring.

RESOURCES: Clay beads: Splendid Loon. Lampworked glass discs: Blue Heeler Glass.

DOTTED SWISS

◎

MATERIALS

2 silver 1½" (3.8 cm) head pins

2 silver 4mm star spacers

1 brown-and-blue 12mm polka-dot clay bead

2 blue 5mm clay donut beads

2 silver 5mm jump rings

1 pair sterling silver ear wires

TOOLS

Flush cutters

Chain-nose pliers

Round-nose pliers

FINISHED SIZE

1¼" (3.2 cm)

1. Use 1 head pin to string 1 silver spacer and 1 polka-dot clay bead.

2. Form a wire-wrapped loop that attaches to 1 clay donut.

3. Attach 1 jump ring to the clay donut.

4. Attach 1 ear wire to the jump ring.

5. Repeat Steps 1 to 4 for the second earring.

RESOURCES: Polka-dot clay beads: Embroidered Soul. Clay donut beads: Joan Miller.

HARDWARE STORE CHIC

○ ○

MATERIALS

9" (22.9 cm) of sterling silver 22-gauge dead-soft wire

7" (17.8 cm) of sterling silver 20-gauge half-hard wire

6 Black Diamond 5mm Swarovski crystal bicones

2 brass 20mm brass pierced washers

TOOLS

Flush cutters

Chain-nose pliers

Round-nose pliers

File or wire smoother

Sharpie

FINISHED SIZE

2" (5.1 cm)

1. Cut the 20-gauge wire in half.

2. Use the 22-gauge wire to make six 1½" (3.8 cm) head pins.

3. Use 1 head pin to string 1 crystal bicone. Form a wrapped loop that attaches to 1 hole in the washer. Repeat to add 2 more dangles, each one adjacent to the previous.

4. Use one 20-gauge wire to form a wrapped loop that attaches to the hole in the washer opposite the middle crystal dangle. Wrap the wire around the Sharpie to make the ear wire. Use the file to smooth the end of the ear wire.

5. Repeat Steps 3 and 4 for the second earring.

RESOURCES: Crystals: Fusionbeads.com. Washers: Stone Mountain.

PENDULUMS

○○○

MATERIALS

28" (71.1 cm) of copper 20-gauge wire

2 amber/green 18mm lampworked glass discs

2 copper 15mm etched rondelles

TOOLS

Flush cutters

Chain-nose pliers

File or wire smoother

Sharpie

FINISHED SIZE

2⅝" (6.7 cm)

1. Cut the wire into two 10" (25.4 cm) pieces and two 4" (10.2 cm) pieces.

2. Use one 10" (25.4 cm) wire to string 1 copper rondelle so that it is 1" (2.5 cm) from one end of the wire. Bend the wire ends so that they cross atop the bead, then bend them straight up.

3. Use the long end of the wire to string 1 lampworked disc, leaving ½" (1.3 cm) between the disc and the copper bead. Bring the wire down around the disc and wrap it sloppily around the middle of the wires.

4. Trim the 1" (2.5 cm) end of wire so as not to show and stick the longer end of wire into the wrap.

5. Use one 4" (10.2 cm) wire to string the lampworked disc so that it is 1" (2.5 cm) from one end of the wire.

6. Wrap the shorter wire end around the neck of the longer wire end and trim.

7. Fold the longer wire end around the Sharpie to make an ear wire. Use the file to smooth the end of the ear wire.

8. Repeat Steps 2 to 7 for the second earring.

RESOURCES: Copper beads: Fusion Beads. Glass discs: Joanne Zekowski.

CLAY POTS

MATERIALS
3" (7.6 cm) of sterling silver 18-gauge dead-soft wire

6" (15.2 cm) of sterling silver 24-gauge dead-soft wire

2 brown 10mm clay round beads

1 pair sterling silver ear wires

TOOLS
Flush cutters

Chain-nose pliers

Ball-peen hammer

Awl

Bench block

FINISHED SIZE
2⅛" (5.4 cm)

1. Cut the 18-gauge wire in half.

2. Hammer flat one end of each wire to splay the end.

3. Use 1" (2.5 cm) of 24-gauge wire to coil around the center of the 18-gauge wire.

4. String 1 clay round bead. Use 2" (5.1 cm) of 24-gauge wire to coil around the 18-gauge wire above the bend.

5. Flatten the other end of the wire to splay.

6. Use the awl to punch a hole in the end of the wire just splayed. Attach 1 ear wire to the hole.

7. Repeat Steps 3 to 6 for the second earring.

RESOURCE: Clay beads: Embroidered Soul.

SIMPLE HOOPS

MATERIALS

7" (17.8 cm) of sterling silver 20-gauge
  dead-soft wire

18 sterling silver 2mm cornerless cubes

TOOLS

Flush cutters

Ring mandrel

Round-nose pliers

Hammer

Bench block

File or wire smoother

FINISHED SIZE

3⅜" (8.6 cm) circumference

1. Cut the wire in half.

2. Use 1 wire to make a loop around size 10 on the ring mandrel, so all the wire is wrapped.

3. Use round-nose pliers to form a simple loop on one end of the wire, making sure the loop is on the same plane as the wire. String 9 cornerless cubes.

4. Where the wire ends of the hoop cross, bend the straight end to 90° and trim to ⅛" (0.3 cm). Use the file to smooth the end.

5. Hammer the sides of the hoop.

6. Repeat Steps 2 to 5 for the second earring.

Alternative: Use size 6° seed beads to add some color.

RESOURCE: Sterling faceted beads: Hands of the Hills.

GET THE SPINS

MATERIALS

6" (15.2 cm) of sterling silver 18-gauge dead-soft wire

16" (40.6 cm) of green 18-gauge craft wire

2 green/blue 25mm lampworked glass discs

1 pair sterling silver ear wires

TOOLS

Flush Cutters

Chain-nose pliers

Round-nose pliers

FINISHED SIZE

1⅜" (3.5 cm)

1. Cut the sterling silver wire in half. Cut the green craft wire in half.

2. Use 1 sterling silver wire to form a spiral using all but ½" (1.3 cm) of wire. Use the remaining ½" (1.3 cm) of wire to form a tiny spiral in the opposite direction of the previous spiral to make an exaggerated S shape.

3. Use chain-nose pliers to grasp 1 green craft wire 2" (5.1 cm) from one end of the wire and make a 90° bend.

4. Form a spiral with the 2" (5.1 cm) length of craft wire.

5. Use the remaining length of craft wire to string the tiny spiral formed in Step 2 and 1 lampworked glass disc.

6. Use round-nose pliers to form a wrapped loop about ⅜" (1 cm) above the glass disc, but do not trim the tail wire. Instead, continue wrapping the wire all the way down the length of wire until it nearly touches the glass bead (about 10 wraps). Trim excess wire. Bend the wrapped length of wire 90° so that it is snug against the back of the glass disc.

7. Attach 1 ear wire to the wrapped loop.

8. Repeat Steps 2 to 7 for the second earring.

RESOURCE: Lampworked glass discs: Kab's Creative Concepts.

Designer Kerry Bogert

KNOTS

⊙⊙⊙

MATERIALS

15' (4.572 m) of sterling silver 24-gauge dead-soft wire

8" (20.3 cm) of sterling silver 20-gauge dead-soft wire

2 green/black 10mm lampworked glass discs

2 sterling silver 7mm jump rings

1 pair sterling silver ear wires

TOOLS

Flush cutters

Coiling Gizmo

Chain-nose pliers

Round-nose pliers

Liver of sulfur (optional)

Disposable cup (optional)

Plastic spoon (optional)

FINISHED SIZE

2⅜" (6 cm)

1. Cut the 24-gauge wire in half. Use the Coiling Gizmo to coil 1 wire to make a 3" (7.6 cm) coil. Repeat with the other wire.

2. Cut the 20-gauge wire in half.

3. Use one 20-gauge wire to form a simple loop. String 1 coil and form a simple loop.

4. Use the coiled piece to form a loose overhand knot.

5. Repeat Steps 3 and 4 to form a second knotted coil. If desired, use liver of sulfur to oxidize the coils.

6. Attach 1 ear wire to the top of 1 coil. Use 1 jump ring to attach 1 disc to the bottom of the coil. Repeat entire step for the second earring.

RESOURCE: Lampworked glass discs: Joanne Zekowski.

MARQUIS

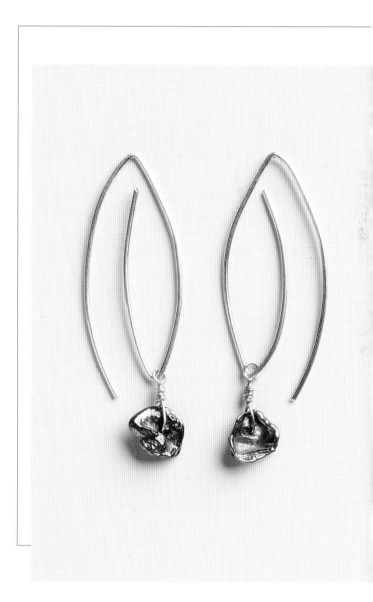

MATERIALS

10" (25.4 cm) of sterling silver 20-gauge half-hard wire

6" (15.2 cm) of sterling silver 26-gauge dead-soft wire

2 peacock blue 8mm center-drilled keishi pearls

TOOLS

Flush cutters

Chain-nose pliers

File or wire smoother

Ruler

FINISHED SIZE

1¾" (4.4 cm)

1. Cut both wires in half.

2. Use chain-nose pliers to make a sharp bend 1½" (3.8 cm) from one end of one 20-gauge wire.

3. Use your fingers to gently curve both halves into arcs.

4. Use chain-nose pliers to make a sharp bend back up toward the center 1¼" (3.2 cm) from the long end of the wire. Gently arc the short length until it touches the other wire at the top of the earring.

5. Use 3" (7.6 cm) of 26-gauge wire and 1 keishi pearl to make a briolette wrapped loop that attaches to the bottom of the earring.

6. Use the file to smooth the end of the earring.

7. Repeat Steps 2 to 6 for the second earring.

RESOURCE: Center-drilled keishi pearls: Abeadstore.com.

TOTEMS

◎

MATERIALS
8" (20.3 cm) of sterling silver 18-gauge dead-soft wire

10 assorted 10mm beads

TOOLS
Flush cutters

Round-nose pliers

File or wire smoother

FINISHED SIZE
1¾" (4.4 cm)

1. Cut the wire in half.

2. Use round-nose pliers to form a simple loop on one end of 1 wire.

3. String 5 beads on the wire and make a sharp 90° angle at the top of the beads.

4. Use your fingers to gently curve the wire into an arc beside the beads. Use the file to smooth the end.

5. Repeat Steps 2 to 4 for the second earring.

Alternative: Use sterling silver 20-gauge wire and pearls for a more delicate look.

RESOURCES: Beads: Joanne Zekowski and Hands of the Hills.

FRESH PICKED FLOWERS

⦾⦾◯

MATERIALS

12" (30.5 cm) of sterling silver 18-gauge dead-soft wire

12" (30.5 cm) of red 20-gauge craft wire

2 red 27mm lampworked glass floral discs

2 yellow with red dots 7×13mm lampworked glass rondelles

1 pair sterling silver ear wires

TOOLS

Flush cutters

¹⁄₁₆" (0.2 cm) mandrel

Chain-nose pliers

Round-nose pliers

FINISHED SIZE

1⅞" (4.8 cm)

1. Cut the 18-gauge wire in half. Use 1 wire to make a spiral head pin. Repeat to make a second head pin.

2. Use the mandrel to coil the 20-gauge wire. Remove the coil from the mandrel, trim the ends, and cut the coil in half. You should have two pieces each about ¾" (1.9 cm) long.

3. Use 1 head pin to string 1 rondelle, 1 floral disc, and 1 piece of coil. Form a wrapped loop, but do not trim the excess wire. Instead, continue to wrap the wire down over the coil. When you reach the glass disc, trim the excess wire.

4. Attach 1 ear wire to the wrapped loop.

5. Repeat Steps 3 and 4 for the second earring.

RESOURCE: Lampworked glass beads: Kab's Creative Concepts.

Designer Kerry Bogert

CHAINED GEMS

○○○

MATERIALS
1½" (3.8 cm) of sterling silver 24-gauge
half-hard or dead-soft wire

5" (12.7 cm) of sterling silver 28-gauge
half-hard or dead-soft wire

2 rutilated quartz 6×8mm faceted rondelles

10 tourmaline 2mm faceted rondelles

6" (15.2 cm) of sterling silver 2×1mm chain

Ear wires

TOOLS
Flush cutters

Chain-nose pliers

Round-nose pliers

Ruler

FINISHED SIZE
2¾" (7 cm)

1. Cut the chain into two ¼" (0.6 cm) lengths, four ½"
(1.3 cm) lengths, two ¾" (1.9 cm) lengths, and two 1"
(2.5 cm) lengths.

2. Cut the 24-gauge wire in half. Cut the 28-gauge wire
into ten 1" (2.5 cm) pieces. Use one 28-gauge wire to
form 1 head pin; repeat to make 6 head pins.

3. Use 1 piece of 24-gauge wire to form a wrapped loop
that attaches to one end each of one ½" (1.3 cm) chain
and one 1" (2.5 cm) chain. String 1 quartz rondelle.
Form a wrapped loop that attaches to the other ends of
the two chains.

4. Use one 28-gauge wire to form a wrapped loop that
attaches to 1 ear wire. String 1 tourmaline and form a
wrapped loop that attaches to the middle link of the ½"
(1.3 cm) chain used in Step 3. Use one 28-gauge wire
to form a wrapped loop that attaches to the middle
link of the 1" (2.5 cm) chain used in Step 3. String 1
tourmaline and form a wrapped loop that attaches to
one end each of one ¼" (0.6 cm) chain, one ½" (1.3 cm)
chain, and one ¾" (1.9 cm) chain.

5. Use 1 head pin to string 1 tourmaline. Form a wrapped
loop that attaches to the other end of the ¼" (0.6 cm)
chain. Repeat using the other ends of the ½" (1.3 cm)
and ¾" (1.9 cm) chains.

6. Repeat Steps 3 to 5 for the second earring.

RESOURCES: Stone beads: House of Gems. Chain: Whim
Beads.

CRYSTALS²

◎

MATERIALS
8" of sterling silver 20-gauge half-hard wire
14 Light Azore Satin 4mm Swarovski crystal bicones

TOOLS
Flush cutters
Round-nose pliers
Flat-nose pliers
File or wire smoother
Ruler
Sharpie

FINISHED SIZE
1⅛" (2.9 cm)

1. Mark ⅝" (1.6 cm) in from one end of a 4" (10.2 cm) piece of wire.

2. Use flat-nose pliers to make a 90° bend at the mark.

3. String 7 crystals from the long end to sit snugly against the bend you just made. Make a 90° bend right after the crystals.

4. Mark ½" (1.3 cm) from one end of the long end of the wire and bend there to complete the square.

5. Use round-nose pliers to bend a hook just above the post and trim the hook to ⅓" (0.8 cm). Use the file to smooth the end of the post.

Alternative: Use four 10mm pearls for everyday earrings.

RESOURCES: Crystals: Fusionbeads.com.

AMPERSANDS

○○

MATERIALS
9" (22.9 cm) of sterling silver 18-gauge dead-soft wire

2 turquoise 10×15mm teardrops

2 sterling silver 7mm triangular jump rings

1 pair sterling silver ear wires

TOOLS
Flush cutters

Chain-nose pliers

Round-nose pliers

Ball-peen hammer

Bench block

FINISHED SIZE
2½" (6.4 cm)

1. Cut the wire in half.

2. Use the hammer to splay one end of 1 wire.

3. With chain-nose pliers and your fingers, bend the splayed end into a 10mm circle and continue to spiral the wire a second time around the first circle.

4. Use the fattest part of the round-nose pliers to bend the "neck" up with a simple loop that attaches to 1 ear wire.

5. Use 1 jump ring to attach 1 turquoise teardrop to the bottom of the earring.

6. Repeat Steps 2 to 5 for the second earring, making sure the second earring is a mirror image of the first.

RESOURCES: Turquoise teardrop beads: Fire Mountain Gems and Beads. Triangular jump rings: Multi Creations Inc.

SWIRLED SWIRLS

○ ○

MATERIALS

12" (30.5 cm) of sterling silver 20-gauge half-hard wire

2 yellow/blue with black swirls 12×8mm lampworked
glass rondelles

TOOLS

Flush cutters

Round-nose pliers

Flat-nose pliers

File or wire smoother

Sharpie

FINISHED SIZE

1⅝" (4.1 cm)

1. Cut two 2" (5.1 cm) pieces of wire; use each wire to
   make 1 head pin. Cut the remaining wire in half.

2. Use round- and flat-nose pliers to make a spiral on one
   end of 1 wire using the last 1¼" (3.2 cm) of wire.

3. Use round-nose pliers to hold the wire about ¼"
   (0.6 cm) from the spiral. Bend the rest of the wire back
   in a U shape next to the spiral.

4. Use the Sharpie as a mandrel to complete the ear wire.
   Use the file to smooth the end.

5. Use 1 head pin to string 1 lampworked glass rondelle.
   Form a wrapped loop. Use the ear wire to string the
   wrapped loop. It should rest in the wire bend formed in
   Step 3.

6. Repeat Steps 2 to 5 for the second earring.

Alternative: Use 14mm Swarovski pearls and gold-filled
wire for elegance.

RESOURCE: Lampworked glass beads: Grace Lampwork Beads
and Jewelry Inc.

POTTERY SHARD PACKAGES

◎

MATERIALS

48" (121.9 cm) of turquoise 22-gauge craft wire

2 turquoise/green 15×20mm pottery shards

1 pair sterling silver ear wires

TOOLS

Flush cutters

Round-nose pliers

Chain-nose pliers

FINISHED SIZE

1½" (3.8 cm)

1. Cut the wire in half.

2. Hold one end of 1 wire against the center back of 1 shard and begin wrapping five times around the width, then twist it to wrap five times around the length, making sure the first end is hidden in the wraps.

3. At the top of the shard, make a wrapped loop, wrapping the round-nose pliers three times to form a triple loop.

4. Attach 1 ear wire to the triple loop.

5. Repeat Steps 2 to 4 for the second earring.

RESOURCE: ParaWire Craft Wire: Paramount Wire Co.

FACETED RINGS

◎◎

MATERIALS

8" (20.3 cm) of silver 26-gauge craft wire

26 sterling silver 3mm cornerless cubes

1 pair sterling silver ear wires

TOOLS

Flush cutters

Chain-nose pliers

Round-nose pliers

FINISHED SIZE

1⅛" (2.9 cm)

1. Cut the wire in half.

2. Use 1 wire to string 13 cornerless cubes to the center of the wire. Use fingers to form the beads and wire into a circle. Tie the ends where the beads meet in a circle, wrapping snugly with one end of the wire between the beads.

3. Use the other end of the wire to form a wrapped loop that attaches to 1 ear wire.

4. Repeat Steps 2 and 3 for the second earring.

RESOURCE: Sterling silver cornerless cubes: Hands of the Hills.

PAISLEY FLORAL

◎

MATERIALS

3" (7.6 cm) of copper 26-gauge wire

2 copper 6×18mm paisley links

2 teal 6mm pressed-glass flowers

1 pair copper ear wires

TOOLS

Flush cutters

Chain-nose pliers

Round-nose pliers

FINISHED SIZE

1⅝" (4.1 cm)

1. Cut the wire in half.

2. Make head pins by spiraling one end of each piece of wire.

3. Use 1 head pin to string 1 flower. Form a wrapped loop that attaches to one end of 1 link.

4. Attach 1 ear wire to the other end of the link.

5. Repeat Steps 3 and 4 for the second earring.

RESOURCE: Copper links: Sunyno.

RUBBER RINGS

○

MATERIALS
8" of purple 20-gauge craft wire
2 black 1" (2.5 cm) rubber O-rings
1 pair sterling silver ear wires

TOOLS
Flush cutters
Round-nose pliers

FINISHED SIZE
1½" (3.8 cm)

1. Cut the wire in half.
2. Use 1 wire to wrap 8 tight coils around 1 rubber O-ring and trim.
3. Use the remaining wire to wrap directly across from the coil made in Step 2. Coil four times and on the fifth wrap, hold the tip of the round-nose pliers next to the ring and wrap around them to form an extended loop. Continue wrapping 4 more wraps around the O-ring and trim.
4. Attach 1 ear wire to the extended loop.
5. Repeat Steps 2 to 4 for the second earring.

Alternative: Wrap a full half of the rubber ring with wire.

RESOURCES: O-rings: Hardware store. ParaWire craft wire: Paramount Wire Co.

CHAIN O' RINGS

○○

MATERIALS

30" (76.2 cm) of Vintage Bronze 24-gauge ParaWire

3" (7.6 cm) of antiqued brass 2×4mm oval chain

10 amber/green 6mm glass whip beads

1 pair bronze ear wires

TOOLS

Flush cutters

Round-nose pliers

FINISHED SIZE

2⅛" (5.4 cm)

1. Cut the wire into ten 3" pieces. Cut the chain in half.

2. Use 1 wire to form a wrapped loop that attaches to 1 glass whip bead. Use the other end of the wire to form a wrapped loop that attaches to one end of 1 chain.

3. Repeat Step 2 twice, for a total of 3 dangles on the end chain link.

4. Repeat Step 2 twice, attaching the second wrapped loop of each dangle to the second-to-last chain link.

5. Attach 1 ear wire to the other end of the chain.

6. Repeat Steps 2 to 5 for the second earring.

Alternative: Sterling chain and 3mm Swarovski beads change these to dramatic evening earrings.

RESOURCES: Glass whip beads: Hanson Stone. Antiqued brass chain: Whimbeads.com.

TANDEM

MATERIALS
12" (30.5 cm) of sterling silver 24-gauge wire

2 aquamarine 5×8mm rondelles

2 aquamarine 6×10mm rondelles

1 pair sterling silver ear wires

TOOLS
Flush cutters

Chain-nose pliers

Round-nose pliers

Liver of sulfur (optional)

Disposable cup (optional)

Plastic spoon (optional)

Polishing pad

FINISHED SIZE
1½" (3.8 cm)

1. Cut the wire in half.

2. Use 1 wire to string one 6×10mm rondelle to the center of the wire. Form a briolette wrapped loop, wrapping one wire around the base of the other wire several times, wrapping up and down about ⅛" (0.3 cm) of the base wire. Trim the excess wrapping wire and use chain-nose pliers to tuck in the wire end.

3. Straighten the base wire and string one 5×7mm rondelle. Use round-nose pliers to form a wrapped loop ⅛" (0.3 cm) from the top of the rondelle. Wrap the wire several times around the base wire. Trim the excess wire and use chain-nose pliers to tuck in the wire end.

4. Attach 1 ear wire to the wrapped loop.

5. Repeat Steps 2 to 4 for the second earring.

6. Use liver of sulfur to oxidize the earrings.

RESOURCES: Sterling silver wire: T.B. Hagstoz. Aquamarine beads: Holy and Pure Gemstones. Ear wires: You and Me Findings. Liver of sulfur, Pro polishing pad: Rio Grande.

Designer Jane Dickerson

KYANITE TEARDROPS

○

MATERIALS
5" (12.7 cm) of sterling silver 20-gauge dead-soft wire

2 kyanite 12×30mm teardrops

2 Thai silver 4mm star spacers

1 pair sterling silver ear wires

TOOLS
Flush cutters

Chain-nose pliers

Round-nose pliers

FINISHED SIZE
1¾" (4.4 cm)

1. Cut the wire in half. Use 1 wire to make 1 head pin; repeat with the other wire.

2. String 1 spacer and 1 kyanite teardrop. Form a wrapped loop and continue wrapping around and down the top of the teardrop to form a bead cap.

3. Trim the wire on the side of the bead so that it will not show from the front or back.

4. Attach 1 ear wire to the wrapped loop.

5. Repeat Steps 2 to 4 for the second earring.

RESOURCE: Kyanite beads: Wrap Stones.

SILVER WHEELS

◎◎

MATERIALS

8" (20.3 cm) of sterling silver 20-gauge half-hard wire

2 sterling silver 10mm bead caps

TOOLS

Flush cutters

Chain-nose pliers

Ball-peen hammer

Bench block

File or wire smoother

Sharpie

FINISHED SIZE

1⅜" (3.5 cm)

1. Cut the wire in half.
2. Use the hammer to flatten the bead caps.
3. Bend a piece of wire in half. Use one end of the wire to string 1 bead cap.
4. Wrap one end of the wire loosely around the other end at the edge of the bead cap.
5. Bend the other wire over the Sharpie to form an ear wire. Use the file to smooth the end of the ear wire.
6. Repeat Steps 2 to 5 for the second earring.

RESOURCE: Bead caps: Anil Kumar.

CONTRADICTION

◎◎

MATERIALS

2 brass 20mm pierced washers

6 white 6mm center-drilled keishi pearls

6 gold-tone 1" (2.5 cm) head pins

1 pair brass ear wires

TOOLS

Chain-nose pliers

FINISHED SIZE

1¼" (3.2 cm)

1. Use 1 head pin to string 1 pearl. Repeat five times.
2. String 1 head pin into one hole in 1 ring. Wrap the wire around and through the hole twice to secure and trim. Repeat twice, placing the pearls in adjacent holes.
3. Attach 1 ear wire to the next hole in the ring.
4. Repeat Steps 2 and 3 for the second earring.

Alternative: Use 4mm stone rondelles for an earthy look.

RESOURCES: Brass pierced washer: Stone Mountain. Center-drilled keishi pearls: Abeadstore.com.

TURQUOISE TRIANGLES

MATERIALS
10" (25.4 cm) of sterling silver 20-gauge half-hard wire

1 turquoise 16×8mm irregularly faceted beads

4 purple size 6° seed beads

1 pair sterling silver ear wires

TOOLS
Flush cutters

Chain-nose pliers

Round-nose pliers

FINISHED SIZE
1⅝" (4.1 cm)

1. Cut the wire in half.

2. Use 1 wire to string 1 seed bead, 1 turquoise bead, and 1 seed bead.

3. Use chain-nose pliers to make a 90° bend beside each seed bead. Push the wire ends together and form a briolette wrapped loop.

4. Attach 1 ear wire to the wrapped loop.

5. Repeat Steps 2 to 4 for the second earring.

Alternative: Use all purple seed beads the length of the bottom of the triangle.

RESOURCE: Turquoise beads: Wrap Stones.

RING-DINGS

MATERIALS

16" (40.6 cm) of olivine 26-gauge craft wire

2 black 1" (2.5 cm) OD ⅛" (0.3 cm) gauge rubber O-rings

2 purple 12mm resin round beads

4 lime-green opaque size 8° seed beads

1 pair copper ear wires

TOOLS

Flush cutters

Chain- or round-nose pliers

FINISHED SIZE

2¼" (5.7 cm)

1. Cut the wire in half.

2. Use 1 wire to string 1 seed bead to the center of the wire. Use pliers to pinch the wire around the seed bead.

3. Use both ends of wire to string 1 resin round bead and 1 seed bead.

4. Separate the 2 wire ends on either side of O-ring. Pull the bauble dangle snug up to the O-ring.

5. Use 1 wire to wrap 7 tight coils around the O-ring, away from the bauble dangle. Repeat with the other wire, wrapping in opposite direction so that the wires are symmetrical on each side of the dangle. Trim wire ends on the same side of the O-ring; this will be the back of the earring.

6. Attach 1 ear wire to the O-ring.

7. Repeat Steps 2 to 6 for the second earring.

RESOURCES: Purple resin beads: Natural Touch Beads. ParaWire craft wire: Paramount Wire Co. O-rings: Local hardware store.

Designer Leslie Rogalski

GONE FISHING

◎

MATERIALS
6" (15.2 cm) of sterling silver 20-gauge half-hard wire

2 sterling silver 18×10mm fish charms

TOOLS
Flush cutters

Round-nose pliers

Ruler

FINISHED SIZE
1⅝" (4.1 cm)

1. Cut the wire in half.

2. Form a simple loop on one end of
   1 wire.

3. Make a bend in the wire 1¾" (4.4 cm) from the simple
   loop. Use your fingers to gently curve both sides.

4. Attach the simple loop to 1 fish charm.

5. Repeat Steps 2 to 4 for the second earring.

RESOURCE: Fish beads: Metalliferous.

WINDING ROADS

◎◎

MATERIALS

18" (45.7 cm) of sterling silver 20-gauge dead-soft wire

2 green 9mm furnace-glass triangle beads

4 silver 4mm star spacers

TOOLS

Flush cutters

Chain-nose pliers

Round-nose pliers

File or wire smoother

Sharpie

FINISHED SIZE

2" (5.1 cm)

1. Cut the wire into two 6" (15.2 cm) pieces and two 3" (7.6 cm) pieces. Use each 3" (7.6 cm) wire to make 1 head pin.

2. Use round-nose pliers to make a simple loop on one end of one 6" (15.2 cm) wire. Make a soft bend above the loop. Move the round-nose pliers ¼" (0.6 cm) from the first bend and bend the wire again in the opposite direction.

3. Move the pliers $3/8$" (1 cm) from the previous bend and bend the wire again in the opposite direction.

4. Repeat Step 3 five times for a total of 7 zigzag bends.

5. Bend the rest of the wire around the Sharpie to make a curve for the ear wire and smooth the end.

6. Use 1 head pin to string 1 spacer, 1 bead, and 1 spacer. Form a wrapped loop that attaches to the loop formed in Step 2.

7. Repeat Steps 2 to 6 for the second earring.

Alternative: Use polymer clay beads for a playful look.

RESOURCE: Furnace-glass beads: Artbeads.com.

COIL WAVES

MATERIALS

12" (30.5 cm) of sterling silver 20-gauge dead-soft wire

TOOLS

Flush cutters

Chain-nose pliers

Round-nose pliers

File or wire smoother

Sharpie

FINISHED SIZE

1½" (3.8 cm)

1. Cut the wire in half.

2. Use round- and chain-nose pliers to create a ⅜" (1 cm) coil on one end of 1 wire.

3. Make a 90° bend with the wire, just above the coil.

4. Use the largest part of the round-nose pliers to grasp the wire just above the bend. Bend the wire to the left, over the top jaw of the pliers, to the 9 o'clock position.

5. Move the pliers to grasp the wire above the last bend. Bend the wire to the right, over the top jaw of the pliers, to 2 o'clock.

6. Grasp the wire with the large part of the pliers, just above the bend. Bend the wire to the left, to 10 o'clock.

7. Grasp the wire with the large part of the pliers, just above the bend. Bend the wire to the right, to 2 o'clock.

8. Use chain-nose pliers to hold the last bend flat. Pull the wire straight back so it is pointing away from you and parallel to your work surface.

9. Bend the wire over the Sharpie to create the ear wire. If the ear wire is too long, use flush cutters to trim it. Use chain-nose pliers to grasp the tip of the ear wire and bend it just slightly away from the earring. Use the file to smooth the tip of the ear wire.

10. Repeat Steps 2 to 9 to create the second earring. Make it a mirror image to the first by making the first bend above the spiral to the right instead of the left.

Designer Jane Dickerson

BARBELLS

MATERIALS

2 sterling silver 20-gauge 1½" (3.8 cm) head pins

10" (25.4 cm) of sterling silver 24-gauge dead-soft wire

4 blue 12mm lampworked glass rondelles

1 pair sterling silver ear wires

TOOLS

Flush cutters

20-gauge mandrel

Chain-nose pliers

Round-nose pliers

FINISHED SIZE

1⅛" (2.9 cm)

1. Use the mandrel to coil the wire. Remove the coil and cut it in half.

2. Use 1 head pin to string 1 bead, 1 coil, and 1 bead. Form a simple loop.

3. Attach 1 ear wire to the simple loop.

4. Repeat Steps 2 and 3 for the second earring.

RESOURCE: Lampworked glass beads: Check your local bead store.

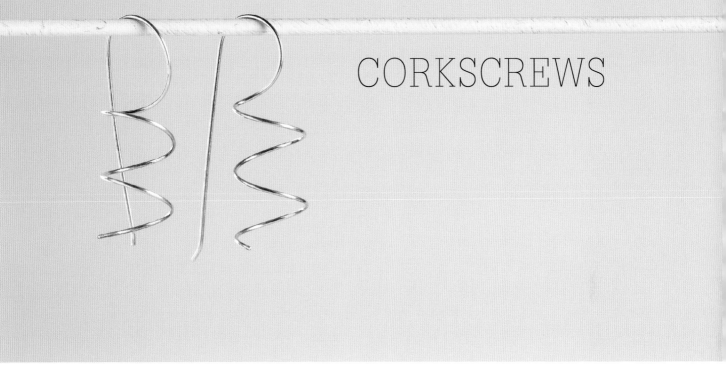

CORKSCREWS

◎
MATERIALS
14" (35.6 cm) of sterling silver 20-gauge half-hard wire

TOOLS
Flush cutters

Large stepped mandrel

Round-nose pliers

File or wire smoother

FINISHED SIZE
1⅞" (4.8 cm)

1. Cut the wire in half.

2. Hold one end of 1 wire against the largest end of the mandrel and wrap 4 complete wraps.

3. Remove the coil from the mandrel and gently pull apart the spiral.

4. To form the ear wire, bend the top ring of the spiral up so the long length of wire bends down.

5. Add a gentle bend to the end of the ear wire. Use the file to smooth the wire end.

6. Repeat Steps 2 to 5 for the second earring.

Alternative: Turn a small loop at the end of the corkscrew and string size 8° seed beads onto the wire to add some color.

CONFETTI

○○○

MATERIALS

24" (61 cm) of silver 28-gauge craft wire

8 fuchsia 5mm square Greek ceramic spacers

6 purple size 6° seed beads

12 silver 4mm sequins

1 pair sterling silver ear wires

TOOLS

Flush cutters

Round-nose pliers

FINISHED SIZE

2⅛" (5.4 cm)

1. Cut the wire into eight 3" (7.6 cm) pieces.

2. Use pliers to hold one piece of wire 1" (2.5 cm) from each end, fold the ends in and cross them over the middle of the piece.

3. Use 1 wire end to string 1 sequin. Use the other wire end to string 1 spacer and 1 sequin.

4. Twist the ends so they wrap around the center of the wire.

5. Repeat Step 2. Use 1 wire end to string 1 sequin and 1 seed bead. Use the other wire end to string 1 spacer and 1 sequin. Repeat Step 4.

6. Repeat Step 2. Use 1 wire end to string 1 sequin, 1 seed bead, and one end of the link formed in the previous step. Use the other wire end to string 1 spacer and 1 sequin.

7. Repeat Step 6.

8. Attach 1 ear wire to one end of the single link and one end of the triple link.

9. Repeat Steps 2 to 8 for the second earring.

RESOURCE: Greek ceramic spacers: Embroidered Soul.

ROUND & ROUND

◎ ◎

MATERIALS
13" (33 cm) of sterling silver 18-gauge dead-soft wire

8" (20.3 cm) of purple 24-gauge craft wire

2 pale blue 8×10mm borosilicate glass drop beads

1 pair sterling silver ear wires

TOOLS
Flush cutters

Ring mandrel

Chain-nose pliers

Round-nose pliers

FINISHED SIZE
2" (5.1 cm)

1. Cut the 18-gauge wire in half. Cut the 24-gauge wire in half.

2. Use round-nose pliers to form a simple loop on one end of one 18-gauge wire.

3. Wrap the long length around size 7 on the ring mandrel two and a half times around, ending across from the simple loop.

4. Form a simple loop on the end of the wire that is on the same plane as the first simple loop. Attach this simple loop to 1 glass drop bead.

5. Attach 1 ear wire to the other simple loop.

6. Use 4" (10.2 cm) of craft wire to wrap around the side of the large ring to hold all the rings in place. Wrap the craft wire snugly, making sure the wraps sit neatly against one another. Use chain-nose pliers to pinch the end of the craft wire tightly against the silver wire.

7. Repeat Steps 2 to 6 for the second earring.

RESOURCES: Borosilicate beads: Unicornebeads.com. ParaWire craft wire: Paramount Wire Co.

PACIFYING EARRINGS

◎

MATERIALS

10" (25.4 cm) of sterling silver 18-gauge dead-soft wire

12" (30.5 cm) of pale turquoise 20-gauge craft wire

2 green/turquoise 15×22mm lampworked glass ring beads with 7mm holes

TOOLS

Flush cutters

Chain-nose pliers

Wire file

Ruler

Sharpie

FINISHED SIZE

1⅞" (4.8 cm)

1. Cut the 18-gauge wire in half. Cut the 20-gauge wire in half.

2. Wrap one 20-gauge wire around one 18-gauge wire, forming a ¾" (1.9 cm) length of coil. Slide the coil so that it is 1¾" (4.4 cm) from one end of the 18-gauge wire and 2½" (6.4 cm) from the other end.

3. Use round-nose pliers to form a bend in the wire at the center of the coil. String 1 lampworked glass bead so that it sits in the bend.

4. Use the short end of wire to wrap around the long end of wire two times just above the end of the coil.

5. Use the Sharpie to bend the long wire into an ear wire, making sure the ear wire is on the same plane as the loop of coiled wire. Trim the wire so that it is about ¾" (1.9 cm) from the arch of the ear wire. Use the file to smooth the wire end.

6. Repeat Steps 2 to 5 for the second earring.

RESOURCE: Lampworked glass beads: Kab's Creative Concepts.

Designer Kerry Bogert

COPPER CRAZY

◎

MATERIALS

4" (10.2 cm) of copper 20-gauge wire

2 antique copper 15mm jump rings

2 copper 8mm large-hole beads

TOOLS

Flush cutters

2 pairs of chain-nose pliers

Round-nose pliers

File or wire smoother

Sharpie

FINISHED SIZE

1⅜" (3.5 cm)

1. Use two pairs of chain-nose pliers, open 1 jump ring. Add the copper bead and close the jump ring.

2. Use round-nose pliers and 2" (5.1 cm) of wire to form a simple loop that attaches to the jump ring.

3. Bend the wire over the Sharpie to shape the ear wire. Grasp the end of the ear wire with chain-nose pliers and bend it slightly away from the earring. Use the file to smooth the end of the ear wire.

4. Repeat Steps 1 to 3 for the second earring.

RESOURCES: Copper over nickel-free brass jump rings: Gems & Findings. Large-hole copper beads: A.F. Silver Design LLC. Copper wire: Metalliferous.

Designer Jane Dickerson

SUMMER FLING

MATERIALS

12" (30.5 cm) of sterling silver 18-gauge wire

2 silver 4mm Smart Beads

2 red 6mm Greek ceramic spacers

2 orange-and-teal 23mm lampworked glass discs

TOOLS

Flush cutters

¼" (0.6 cm) mandrel

Chain-nose pliers

Round-nose pliers

Ball-peen hammer

Bench block

Ruler

Sharpie

FINISHED SIZE

1⅝" (4.1 cm)

Note: Smart Beads are silicone-lined beads designed to stay where you put them. Using a Smart Bead will keep it from floating up the bends of the wire and possibly coming off the ear hook part of the earring.

1. Use round-nose pliers to form a wrapped loop about 1" (2.5 cm) from the end of one 6" (15.2 cm) piece of wire.

2. String 1 glass disc, 1 ceramic spacer, and 1 Smart Bead.

3. Form a 90° angle in the wire against the Smart Bead.

4. Make a mark on the wire 1" (2.5 cm) from the bend. Center the mark on the mandrel and bend the wire over the mandrel to form the ear wire.

5. Line up the straight length of wire with the wrapped loop. Trim the wire to ⅛" (0.3 cm) past the loop. The wire end should now be able to slip into the wrapped loop. Use the file to smooth the wire end.

6. Hammer the rounded hook of your earrings to slightly flatten and work-harden the bend in the wire.

7. Repeat Steps 1 to 6 for the second earring.

RESOURCES: Smart Beads: Jewelry Supply. Greek ceramic beads: The Mykonos.

Designer Kerry Bogert

ENTANGLED

○○
MATERIALS

24" (61 cm) of sterling silver 20-gauge dead-soft wire

2 green 10mm furnace-glass triangle beads

2 green 10mm furnace-glass square beads

1 pair sterling silver ear wires

TOOLS

Flush cutters

Chain-nose pliers

Round-nose pliers

FINISHED SIZE

2⅛" (5.4 cm)

1. Cut the wire in half.

2. Bend 1 wire around the round-nose pliers to make a U shape 3" (7.6 cm) from one end of the wire.

3. String 1 square bead and cross the wires above the bead.

4. Use the longer end of wire to sloppily wrap about the crossed wires five or six times until both ends of the wire are the same length.

5. Use 1 end of the wire to string 1 triangle bead. Use the other end of the wire to pass through the same bead in the opposite direction.

6. Form a briolette wrapped loop above the second bead.

7. Attach 1 ear wire to the wrapped loop.

8. Repeat Steps 2 to 7 for the second earring.

RESOURCE: Furnace-glass beads: Artbeads.com.

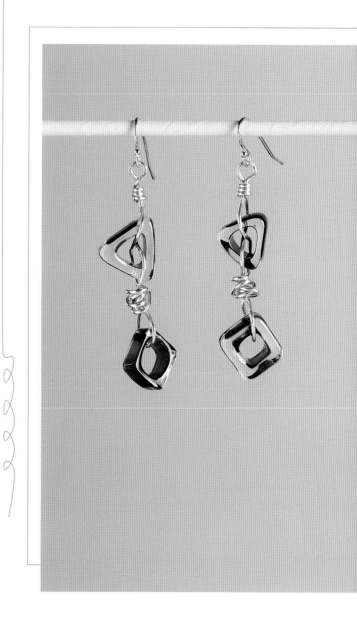

MOBILES

◎

MATERIALS
9" (22.9 cm) of copper 18-gauge wire
1 pair copper ear wires

TOOLS
Flush cutters
Round-nose pliers
Flat-nose pliers
Ball-peen hammer
Bench block

FINISHED SIZE
1¾" (4.4 cm)

1. Cut the wire in half.
2. Use one end of 1 wire to form a spiral with 3 complete coils.
3. Use the widest part of the jaw of round-nose pliers to form a loop ¼" (0.6 cm) from the coil.
4. Repeat Step 2 on the other end of the wire.
5. Use the hammer to flatten the spirals.
6. Attach 1 ear wire to the loop.
7. Repeat Steps 2 to 6 for the second earring.

PRIMITIVE WHEELS

MATERIALS

10" (25.4 cm) of sterling silver 18-gauge dead-soft wire

2 Bali silver 12mm wheel beads

TOOLS

Flush cutters

Large stepped mandrel

Chain-nose pliers

Round-nose pliers

File or wire smoother

FINISHED SIZE

1⅝" (4.1 cm)

1. Cut the wire in half.

2. Use round-nose pliers to make a ⅛" (0.3 cm) gentle bend on one end of 1 wire. Use the file to smooth the end.

3. Bend the wire halfway around the largest step on the mandrel, then bend the bottom of the wire halfway around the mandrel to form an oval. One-half inch from that bend, fold the wire over the largest step on the mandrel, in the opposite direction of the bend.

4. String 1 bead and make a double-wrapped loop opposite the bend made in Step 2.

5. Repeat Steps 2 to 4 for the second earring.

Alternative: Use small lampworked glass disc beads for an artisan look.

RESOURCE: Bali silver wheel beads: Hands of the Hills.

TURNING PURPLE

MATERIALS

12" (30.5 cm) of purple 20-gauge craft wire

2 copper 14mm jump rings

2 copper 20mm jump rings

1 pair copper ear wires

TOOLS

Flush cutters

Chain-nose pliers

Round-nose pliers

FINISHED SIZE

1⅞" (4.8 cm)

1. Cut the wire in half.

2. Make sure the jump rings are closed as tightly as possible. Use your pliers as needed to adjust.

3. Use your fingers to wrap 1 wire around one 20mm jump ring, coiling the wire around the ring seven times.

4. Hold one 14mm jump ring next to the partially wrapped 20mm jump ring. Make 3 wraps around both rings. The rings should be snug together but not overlap.

5. Repeat Step 3. Trim excess purple wire.

6. Use your fingers to turn the copper rings inside the coiled purple wire so the gaps are hidden within the purple coils. The rings will be snug but will slide.

7. Attach 1 ear wire to the 14mm jump ring.

8. Repeat Steps 3 to 7 for the second earring.

RESOURCES: Copper connectors, ear wires, and jump rings: Gems and Findings. ParaWire craft wire: Paramount Wire Co.

Designer Leslie Rogalski

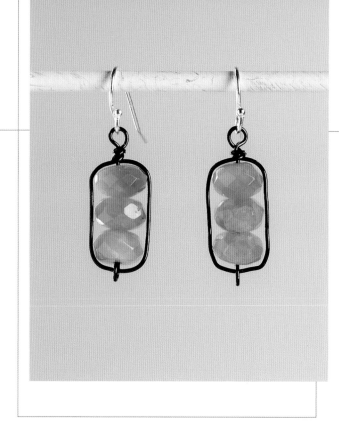

FRAMED

◎

MATERIALS

6" (15.2 cm) of blue 22-gauge craft wire

6 blue quartz 8mm faceted rondelles

1 pair sterling silver ear wires

TOOLS

Flush cutters

Chain-nose pliers

Round-nose pliers

FINISHED SIZE

1¼" (3.2 cm)

1. Cut the wire in half.

2. Use 1 wire to form a simple loop at one end. String 3 rondelles and begin to make a wrapped loop. Wrap the tail wire around the neck only once.

3. Bend the wire around and down the stack of beads, threading the end of the wire through the simple loop. Wrap the wire up the other side of the stack of beads and complete the wrap around the neck of the wrapped loop.

4. Attach 1 ear wire to the wrapped loop.

5. Repeat Steps 2 to 4 for the second earring.

Alternative: Use sterling wire and black pearls.

RESOURCE: Blue quartz beads: House of Gems.

SIMPLE FLOWERS

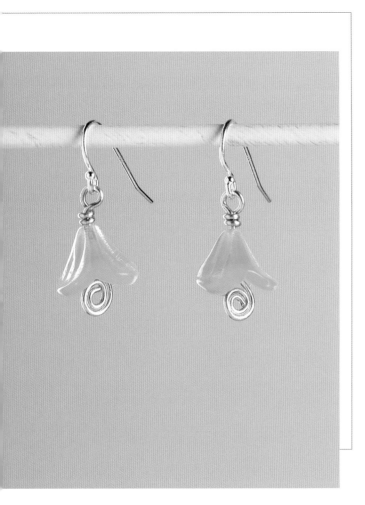

◎

MATERIALS

5½" (14 cm) of sterling silver 20-gauge
   dead-soft wire

2 pressed-glass 7×12mm bell flower beads

1 pair sterling silver ear wires

TOOLS

Flush cutters

Chain-nose pliers

Round-nose pliers

FINISHED SIZE

1" (2.5 cm)

1. Cut the wire in half.

2. Use round-nose pliers and chain-nose pliers to make a 5mm spiral on one end of each wire.

3. Use 1 wire to string 1 flower bead and form a wire-wrapped loop. Repeat for the second earring.

4. Attach ear wires.

RESOURCE: Pressed-glass bell flower beads: Artbeads.com.

LITTLE GEMS

◎

MATERIALS

2 sterling silver 26-gauge 1" (2.5 cm) head pins

2 soldered links from a sterling silver 24-gauge 10mm round chain

2 labradorite 8mm cubed faceted cubes

1 pair sterling silver ear wires

TOOLS

Flush cutters

Round-nose pliers

FINISHED SIZE

1⅛" (2.9 cm)

1. Slip 1 soldered round link over both jaws of the round-nose pliers and gently open the jaws to stretch the ring into an oval.

2. Use 1 head pin to string 1 cube. Form a wrapped loop that attaches to the oval.

3. Attach 1 ear wire to the oval.

4. Repeat Steps 1 to 3 for the second earring.

Alternative: For an elegant earring, use gold rings and pearl beads.

RESOURCE: Labradorite cubes: Anil Kumar.

ORBITAL

○ ○

MATERIALS

8" (20.3 cm) of sterling silver 20-gauge half-hard wire

2 stone 11mm coin beads

TOOLS

Flush cutters

Chain-nose pliers

File or wire smoother

FINISHED SIZE

⅝" (1.6 cm) beaded earring front,
1½" (3.8 cm) earring post

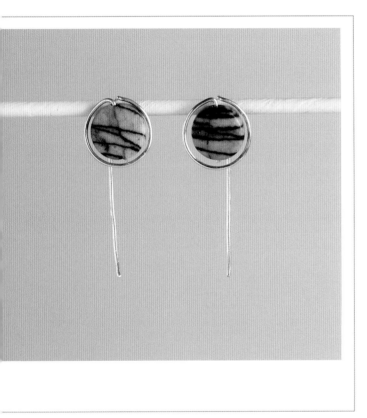

1. Cut the wire in half.

2. Use chain-nose pliers to make a tiny bend at one end of 1 wire. String 1 stone coin onto the short bend.

3. Use fingers to wrap the wire around the circumference of the stone coin.

4. Use chain-nose pliers to make a 90° bend at the top of the stone, perpendicular to the previous bend.

5. Use your fingers to gently curve the ear wire. Trim the length of the ear wire as desired. Use the file to smooth the wire end.

6. Repeat Steps 2 to 5 for the second earring.

Alternative: Use shank buttons and hook the wire into the shank to start.

RESOURCE: Stone beads: Fire Mountain Gems and Beads.

LONG ROUNDS

◎

MATERIALS

11" (27.9 cm) of sterling silver 20-gauge half-hard wire

2 purple 20mm lampworked glass donuts

TOOLS

Flush cutters

Large stepped mandrel

Round-nose pliers

File or wire smoother

FINISHED SIZE

2⅝" (6.7 cm)

1. Cut the wire in half.
2. At 1¼" (3.2 cm) from one end of 1 wire, bend the wire over the smallest step on the mandrel.
3. At 2" (5.1 cm) from the first bend, make a second bend around the largest step on the mandrel.
4. Use round-nose pliers to make a small bend outward at the top end. Use the file to smooth the end.
5. On the bottom end, make a small simple loop for the catch.
6. String 1 donut.
7. Repeat Steps 2 to 6 for the second earring.

Alternative: Use a ¾" (1.9 cm) turquoise stone donut for a Southwestern look.

RESOURCE: Lampworked glass beads: Beads of Passion.

GOING GREEN

MATERIALS

2" (5.1 cm) of sterling silver 16-gauge
dead-soft wire

2 green 14mm glass rings

1 pair sterling silver ear wires

TOOLS

Flush cutters

8mm mandrel

Chain-nose pliers

Ball-peen hammer

Bench block

FINISHED SIZE

1¼" (3.2 cm)

1. Coil the wire around the 8mm mandrel.

2. Cut the coils into jump rings.

3. Use the hammer and bench block to flatten the jump rings. Close up any gap after hammering.

4. Attach 1 jump ring to 1 glass ring. Attach 1 ear wire to the jump ring.

5. Repeat Step 4 for the second earring.

Alternative: Dangle another hammered silver ring instead of glass.

RESOURCE: Green glass rings: Sunyno.

DOUBLE SILVER CIRCLES

⊙⊙

MATERIALS
10" (25.4 cm) of sterling silver 18-gauge dead-soft wire

2 Bali silver 10×12mm beads

1 pair sterling silver flat-front ear wires

TOOLS
Flush cutters

Ring mandrel

Round-nose pliers

Hammer

Bench block

FINISHED SIZE
2⅝" (6.7 cm)

1. Cut the wire in half.

2. Use the ring mandrel at size 4 to form a wrapped loop with one end of 1 wire.

3. String 1 bead.

4. Use the fattest part of your round-nose pliers to form a wrapped loop.

5. Use the hammer to flatten both loops.

6. Attach 1 ear wire to the small loop.

7. Repeat Steps 2 to 6 for the second earring.

Alternative: Use 8mm round lampwork beads for an artisan look.

RESOURCE: Bali beads: Multi Creations Inc.

BLACK+WHITE+RED ALL OVER

MATERIALS
2 black 12mm wooden rings

2 painted 15mm plastic discs

2 silver 3mm jump rings

2 silver 5mm jump rings

2 silver 7mm jump rings

1 pair sterling silver ear wires

TOOLS
2 pairs of chain-nose pliers

FINISHED SIZE
1½" (3.8 cm)

1. Attach one 3mm jump ring to the top of 1 disc. Use one 5mm jump ring to attach the 3mm jump ring to 1 ear wire.

2. Use one 7mm jump ring to attach the bottom hole of the disc to 1 wooden ring.

3. Repeat Steps 1 and 2 for the second earring.

Alternative: Dangle a Swarovski crystal from the bottom of the ring for sparkle.

RESOURCES: Plastic discs: My Elements. Wooden rings: Michaels.

UNEXPECTED

◎

MATERIALS

2" (5.1 cm) of sterling silver 16-gauge dead-soft wire

2" (5.1 cm) of sterling silver 24-gauge dead-soft wire

2 center-drilled 8mm keishi pearls

1 pair sterling silver ear wires

TOOLS

Flush cutters

Chain-nose pliers

Round-nose pliers

Ball-peen hammer

Awl

Bench block

FINISHED SIZE

1¾" (4.4 cm)

1. Cut the 16-gauge wire in half. Cut the 24-gauge wire in half.

2. Use the hammer to flatten both pieces of 16-gauge wire. Use the ball end of the hammer to texture the 16-gauge wires.

3. Use the awl and hammer to pierce a hole near both ends of both pieces.

4. Use 1 piece of 24-gauge wire and 1 pearl to form a briolette loop that attaches to one hole of one 16-gauge wire. Attach 1 ear wire to the other hole.

5. Repeat Step 4 for the second earring.

Alternative: Use Swarovski crystals for some bling!

RESOURCE: Center-drilled keishi pearls: Abeadstore.com.

RAKU BRICKS

◎

MATERIALS
6" (15.2 cm) of sterling silver 18-gauge dead-soft wire
2 white 10×15mm raku brick beads
1 pair sterling silver ear wires

TOOLS
Flush cutters
Round-nose pliers
Flat-nose pliers

FINISHED SIZE
1⅝" (4.1 cm)

1. Cut the wire in half.
2. Make a spiral at the end of 1 wire. String 1 raku bead and form a simple loop.
3. Attach 1 ear wire to the simple loop.
4. Repeat Steps 2 and 3 for the second earring.

RESOURCE: Raku brick beads: Flamin' Turtle.

BLACK MOONS

◎ ◎

MATERIALS

24" (61 cm) of dark annealed steel 19-gauge wire

2 lava 10mm round beads with inlaid Swarovski crystals

1 pair gold-filled ear wires

TOOLS

Heavy-duty wire cutters

Ring mandrel

Round-nose pliers

FINISHED SIZE

2½" (6.4 cm)

1. Cut the wire into two 9" (22.9 cm) pieces and two 3" (7.6 cm) pieces.

2. Use round-nose pliers to form a simple loop on one end of one 9" (22.9 cm) wire.

3. Wrap the long length around size 10 on the ring mandrel two and a half times around, ending across from the simple loop.

4. Form a simple loop on the end of the wire that is perpendicular to the first simple loop.

5. Use one 3" (7.6 cm) piece of wire to make a head pin. String 1 bead and form a simple loop that attaches to the simple loop formed in the previous step.

6. Attach 1 ear wire to the loop formed in Step 2.

7. Repeat Steps 2 to 6 for the second earring.

Alternative: Use 8mm Swarovski crystals for even more sparkle!

RESOURCE: Lava beads: Fire Mountain Gems.

ARCHEOLOGICAL DIGS

MATERIALS
6" (15 cm) of sterling silver 20-gauge half-hard wire

6 seed-pod beads

2 bell charms

TOOLS
Flush cutters

Round-nose pliers

File or wire smoother

Sharpie

FINISHED SIZE
1¾" (4.4 cm)

1. Cut wire in half.

2. Make a simple loop on one end.

3. Attach a bell charm in the simple loop.

4. Thread on 3 seed-pod beads.

5. Bend the wire over a sharpie to form the ear wire and smooth the end.

6. Repeat for the second earring.

Alternative: Use Swarovski crystals instead of the bell charms for some bling!

RESOURCES: Bell charms: Bead Paradise II. Seed-pod beads: Columbian crafts.

BELL FLOWERS

○ ○

MATERIALS

3" (7.6 cm) of sterling silver 20-gauge dead-soft wire

4" (10.2 cm) of sterling silver 1×3mm oval chain

6 silver 26-gauge 1½" (3.8 cm) head pins

2 Thai silver 10mm flower bead caps

4 Montana blue 4mm crystal bicones

2 Bali silver 4mm Bali beads

1 pair sterling silver ear wires

TOOLS

Flush cutters

Chain-nose pliers

Round-nose pliers

FINISHED SIZE

1¾" (4.4 cm)

1. Cut the wire in half. Cut the chain into four ¾" (1.9 cm) pieces and two ½" (1.3 cm) pieces.

2. Use 1 head pin to string 1 crystal bicone. Form a wrapped loop that attaches to one ¾" (1.9 cm) chain. Use 1 head pin to string 1 crystal bicone. Form a wrapped loop that attaches to one ½" (1.3 cm) chain. Use 1 head pin to string 1 silver bead. Form a wrapped loop that attaches to one ¾" (1.9 cm) chain.

3. Use 1 wire to form a simple loop that attaches to the other ends of the chains used in the previous step. String 1 bead cap and form a wrapped loop that attaches to 1 ear wire.

4. Repeat Steps 2 and 3 for the second earring.

RESOURCE: Thai silver flower end caps: Hands of the Hills.

CELTIC CURLS

○○

MATERIALS
12" (30.5 cm) of copper 14-gauge wire

2 copper 8mm corrugated hollow beads

1 pair copper ear wires

TOOLS
Flush cutters

Chain-nose pliers

Round-nose pliers

Ball-peen hammer

Bench block

FINISHED SIZE
1¾" (4.4 cm)

1. Cut the wire in half.

2. Use round- and chain-nose pliers to make a clockwise spiral on one end of 1 wire.

3. String 1 copper bead.

4. Use round- and chain-nose pliers to make a counterclockwise spiral, the same size as the first spiral, at the other end of the wire to form an S shape.

5. Use the ball end of the hammer to add a subtle texture in the spirals, avoiding the copper bead.

6. Use pliers to gently bring the spirals in close to the copper bead.

7. Attach 1 ear wire to 1 spiral.

8. Repeat Steps 2 to 7 for the second earring, attaching the ear wire so the spirals mirror each other when worn.

RESOURCES: Copper ear wires and jump rings: Gems and Findings. Copper beads: A.F. Silver Design, LLC.

Designer Leslie Rogalski

SWITCHING GEARS

○○

MATERIALS

16" (40.6 cm) of sterling silver 20-gauge dead-soft wire

2 purple 18mm lampworked glass discs

6 purple 6mm square Greek ceramic spacers

1 pair sterling silver ear wires

TOOLS

Flush cutters

Round-nose pliers

Liver of sulfur (optional)

Disposable cup (optional)

Plastic spoon (optional)

FINISHED SIZE

2⅛" (5.4 cm)

1. Cut the wire in half.

2. Use 1 wire to string 1 lampworked glass disc 1½" (3.8 cm) from one end of 1 wire.

3. Bend the wires up and sloppily wrap the long end around the short end right above the disc bead. Tuck the end into the nest of wire to hide it.

4. Use the remaining wire to string 3 spacers. Form a wrapped loop that attaches to 1 ear wire.

5. Repeat Steps 2 to 4 for the second earring.

6. Use liver of sulfur to oxidize the earrings.

RESOURCES: Ceramic spacer beads: Embroidered Soul. Lampworked glass disc beads: Blue Heeler Glass.

TRAPEZE

◎

MATERIALS

10" (25.4 cm) of sterling silver 20-gauge half-hard wire

2 dark blue 10×12mm clay pillow beads

1 pair sterling silver ear wires

TOOLS

Flush cutters

Chain-nose pliers

Round-nose pliers

FINISHED SIZE

2⅜" (6 cm)

1. Cut the wire in half.

2. Use 1 wire to string 1 bead to the center of the wire. Use your fingers to bend each wire up against the ends of the bead.

3. Use round-nose pliers to form a simple loop on each end of the wire. Bend one loop over to 90° and hook it around the neck of the other wire.

4. Attach 1 ear wire to the remaining simple loop.

5. Repeat Steps 2 to 4 for the second earring.

RESOURCE: Clay pillow beads: Eclectica.

COILED COILS

◎ ◎

MATERIALS

5' (12.7 cm) of sterling silver 24-gauge dead-soft wire

6" (15.2 cm) of sterling silver 18-gauge dead-soft wire

2 sterling silver 5mm jump rings

2 sterling silver 24-gauge head pins

2 smokey quartz 5×10mm center-drilled briolettes

1 pair sterling silver ear wires

TOOLS

Flush cutters

18-gauge steel mandrel

⅜" (1 cm) wooden dowel

Round-nose pliers

FINISHED SIZE

2⅛" (5.4 cm)

1. Cut the 18-gauge wire in half.
2. Coil the 24-gauge wire around the steel mandrel to make 4¾" (12.1 cm) of coil. Remove the coil from the mandrel and cut it in half.
3. Use round-nose pliers to form a simple loop on one end of 1 wire. String 1 coil and form a simple loop. Wrap the wire/coil around the wood mandrel.
4. Bend the simple loops out to 90°. Use 1 jump ring to attach 1 ear wire to 1 simple loop.
5. Use 1 head pin to string 1 briolette. Form a wrapped loop that attaches to the other simple loop.
6. Repeat Steps 3 to 5 for the second earring.

RESOURCE: Smokey quartz briolettes: Wrap Stones.

COPPER CORKSCREWS

○

MATERIALS
16" (40.6 cm) of copper 20-gauge dead-soft wire

TOOLS
Flush cutters

Round-nose pliers

File or wire smoother

FINISHED SIZE
1⅛" (2.9 cm)

1. Cut the wire in half.
2. Use round-nose pliers to hold one end of 1 wire at the base of the pliers. Wrap the wire up the jaw to form 9 coils.
3. Remove the wire and gently spread the coils and curve them into an arc.
4. Use your fingers to bend the remaining wire into half a hoop.
5. Bend the largest coil up to serve as the loop for the hook. Trim the hoop to just below the loop and use round-nose pliers to gently curve the end into the hook. Use the file to smooth the end of the wire.
6. Repeat Steps 2 to 5 for the second earring.

FLOURISH

◎◎◎

MATERIALS

20" (50.8 cm) of annealed steel 19-gauge wire

2 red 6mm glass rounds

1 pair gunmetal ear wires

TOOLS

Flush cutters

Chain-nose pliers

Round-nose pliers

Ball-peen hammer

Bench block

FINISHED SIZE

2¾" (7 cm)

1. Cut the wire in half.

2. Use 4" (10.2 cm) of the end of 1 wire to make a spiral on one end of 1 wire.

3. Use round-nose pliers to make a small loop even with the outer edge of the spiral; grasp the wire with pliers where you want the loop to sit, and use your fingers to bend the wire under the nose of the pliers, forming a loop.

4. Bring the wire to the opposite side of the large spiral slightly farther from the spiral than the loop just made. Repeat Step 3 to form a second loop. Repeat Step 3 again to form a third loop, leaving a distance between it and the first loop so your second loop is centered between the first and third loop. Bend the wire tail so that it is perpendicular to the center of the spiral.

5. Hammer the loops and spiral to flatten slightly, making sure to avoid hammering the wire tail. Trim the tail to 1" (2.5 cm).

6. String 1 red bead down to the loop. Use round-nose pliers to make a small spiral, on the same plane as, but in the opposite direction of the spiral formed in Step 3. Carefully hammer the small spiral, avoiding the bead.

7. Attach 1 ear wire to the outer loop of the small spiral.

8. Repeat Steps 2 to 7 for the second earring, creating a mirror image of the first earring.

RESOURCE: Ear wires: Artbeads.com.

Designer Leslie Rogalski

NISSHU

MATERIALS

5" (12.7 cm) of sterling silver 24-gauge dead-soft wire

2 antiqued silver-plated 8×12mm Nisshu charms

1 pair sterling silver ear wires

TOOLS

Flush cutters

Chain-nose pliers

Round-nose pliers

Liver of sulfur (optional)

Disposable cup (optional)

Plastic spoon (optional)

Polishing pad

FINISHED SIZE

1⅜" (3.5 cm)

1. Cut the wire in half.

2. Thread 1" (2.5 cm) of 1 of wire through the charm. Cross the wires above the charm, as if you were forming a briolette wrapped loop. Wrap the short wire around the long wire.

3. Straighten the long wire. Use round-nose pliers to begin a wrapped loop, leaving ¼" (0.6 cm) above the charm for wrapping space. Wrap the wire up and down the stem, over the wrap from Step 2. Trim the excess wire and use chain-nose pliers to tuck the wire end into the wrapped wire.

4. Attach 1 ear wire to the wrapped loop.

5. Repeat Steps 2 to 4 for the second earring.

6. Use liver of sulfur to antique the earrings. Use the polishing pad to remove any excess patina and polish the wire.

RESOURCES: Nisshu charms: TierraCast (wholesale only). Sterling silver wire: T.B. Hagstoz. Ear wires: You and Me Findings. Liver of sulfur: Rio Grande.

Designer Jane Dickerson

ENVY

MATERIALS

13' (3.96 m) of sterling silver 24-gauge dead-soft wire

2 sterling silver 4mm silver jump rings

2 sterling silver 6mm silver jump rings

6 green 12mm glass rings

1 pair sterling silver ear wires

TOOLS

Flush cutters

Coiling Gizmo

Chain-nose pliers

Liver of sulfur (optional)

Disposable cup (optional)

Plastic spoon (optional)

FINISHED SIZE

2" (5.1 cm)

1. Cut the wire in half.

2. Use the smaller mandrel in the Coiling Gizmo to coil both pieces of wire.

3. Use chain-nose pliers to lift up the last coil on both ends of 1 coil to a 90° angle from the coil.

4. String 3 glass rings onto the coil. Press the ends of the coil together so the lifted rings meet, twisting the rings if necessary.

5. Attach one 4mm jump ring to the two lifted rings. Use one 6mm jump ring to attach 1 ear wire to the 4mm jump ring.

6. Repeat Steps 3 to 5 for second earring.

7. Use liver of sulfur to oxidize the earrings, if desired.

RESOURCE: Glass rings: Sunyno.

EASY HOOPS

○

MATERIALS
9" (12.7 cm) of sterling silver 20-gauge half-hard wire

2 lampworked glass 8×16mm beads

TOOLS
Flush cutters

Ring mandrel

Round mandrel

Chain-nose pliers

Round-nose pliers

File or wire smoother

Ruler

Sharpie

FINISHED SIZE
1⅛" (2.9 cm)

1. Cut the wire in half.

2. Use round-nose pliers to create a simple loop on one end of 1 wire.

3. Place the loop flat against the ring mandrel at size 7 and wrap the wire around to form a complete circle. Use the Sharpie to mark the point where the wire completes the circle and crosses the center of the loop.

4. Cut the end of the wire ¼" (0.6 cm) longer than the mark made in Step 3. String 1 lampworked glass bead onto the hoop.

5. Use chain-nose pliers to grasp the tip of the wire end and bend it slightly away from the earring. Use the file to smooth the end of the ear wire. Place the wire tail into the loop to close.

6. Repeat Steps 2 to 5 for the second earring.

RESOURCES: Lampworked glass beads: Jay Chantell. Sterling silver wire: T.B. Hagstoz.

Designer Jane Dickerson

PEBBLES

MATERIALS

1" (2.5 cm) of sterling silver 3mm rolo chain

2 sterling silver 7mm square jump rings

2 top-drilled 12×20mm pebbles

1 pair sterling silver ear wires

TOOLS

Flush cutters

2 pairs of chain-nose pliers

Liver of sulfur (optional)

Disposable cup (optional)

Plastic spoon (optional)

FINISHED SIZE

1⅛" (2.9 cm)

1. Cut the rolo chain in half.

2. Use 1 jump ring to attach 1 pebble to one end of 1 piece of chain. Attach 1 ear wire to the other end of the chain.

3. Repeat Step 2 for the second earring.

4. Use liver of sulfur to oxidize the earrings.

RESOURCES: Pebbles: Riverstone Bead Company. Square jump rings: Multi Creations Inc.

SUMMER BLOOMS

○○

MATERIALS
7½" (19.1 cm) of sterling silver 20-gauge half-hard wire

2 yellow 8mm Lucite flower beads

2 blue 8mm Lucite flower beads

1 pair sterling silver ear wires

TOOLS
Flush cutters

Round-nose pliers

Flat-nose pliers

Ball-peen hammer

Bench block

FINISHED SIZE
1⅞" (4.8 cm)

1. Cut the wire in half.

2. Use round-nose pliers to make a tiny loop at one end of 1 wire.

3. String 1 yellow flower bead and bend the wire straight up against the back of the bead to hold the flower snugly against the loop.

4. Place flat-nose pliers 1½" (3.8 cm) up from the flower and make a 45° bend. Use your fingers to gently curve each side into a gentle arc.

5. Repeat Step 3 using 1 blue flower bead and the other end of the wire.

6. Gently hook the second flower over the first to complete the marquis shape.

7. Hammer the wire lightly with a ball-peen hammer.

8. Attach 1 ear wire to the 45° bend.

9. Repeat Steps 2 to 8 for the second earring.

Alternative: Use green craft wire to look like stems.

RESOURCE: Plastic flower beads: Black Sheep Beads.

RINGS OF GLASS

MATERIALS
4" (10.2 cm) of sterling silver 20-gauge half-hard wire

2 teal 15mm glass rings

TOOLS
Flush cutters

Round-nose pliers

File or wire smoother

Sharpie

FINISHED SIZE
1⅛" (2.9 cm)

1. Cut the wire in half.

2. Use round-nose pliers in the middle of the jaw to make a simple loop on one end of 1 wire.

3. Use the Sharpie to shape an ear wire. Use the file to smooth the end.

4. Attach the loop to 1 glass ring.

5. Repeat Steps 2 to 4 for the second earring.

Alternative: Hang hammered closed jump rings for an everyday earring.

RESOURCE: Glass rings: Sunyno.

SILVERED SATURNS

◎

MATERIALS

2" (5.1 cm) of sterling silver 20-gauge half-hard wire

2 red 10mm lampworked glass rondelles

4 copper size 6° seed beads

1 pair sterling silver ear wires

TOOLS

Flush cutters

Round-nose pliers

Ball-peen hammer

Bench block

FINISHED SIZE

1⅛" (2.9 cm)

1. Cut the wire in half.

2. Use the hammer and bench block to create a flat paddle at one end of 1 piece of wire.

3. Use round-nose pliers to curl the flattened paddle into a loop.

4. String 1 seed bead, 1 lampworked glass rondelle, and 1 seed bead; form a simple loop that attaches to 1 ear wire.

5. Repeat Steps 2 to 4 for the second earring.

RESOURCES: Sterling wire: T.B. Hagstoz. Lampworked glass beads: Blue Heeler Beads.

Designer Jane Dickerson

FRIVOLOUSLY FRINGED

○○

MATERIALS

10" (25.4 cm) of turquoise 10-gauge craft wire

10" (25.4 cm) of purple 10-gauge craft wire

2" (5.1 cm) of sterling silver 3×4mm oval chain

2 sterling silver 1" (2.5 cm) head pins

2 sterling silver 4mm round beads

6 teal purple-lined size 8° seed beads

2 fuchsia 4mm Greek ceramic spacers

2 teal 4mm Greek ceramic spacers

2 purple with turquoise dots 25mm lampworked glass discs

1 pair sterling silver ear wires

TOOLS

Flush cutters

¼" (0.6 cm) mandrel

Chain-nose pliers

Round-nose pliers

FINISHED SIZE

1⅞" (4.8 cm)

1. Cut the chain in half.

2. Make the jump rings. Wrap the turquoise wire around the mandrel to coil the wire. Use flush cutters to cut the coil into 12 jump rings. Repeat with the purple wire.

3. Use 1 head pin to string 1 sterling round bead and 1 glass disc. Form a wrapped loop that attaches to one end of 1 chain.

4. Attach 1 ear wire to the other end of the chain.

5. Add the fringe. Use 6 turquoise jump rings, 6 purple jump rings, 3 seed beads, 1 fuchsia spacer, and 1 teal spacer to form the fringe. Attach 2 to 3 jump rings to each chain link, except for the link containing the wrapped loop, randomly placing the beads and spacers on the jump rings.

6. Repeat Steps 3 to 5 for the second earring.

RESOURCES: Chain: Rio Grande. Sterling silver round beads: Jewelry Supply. Seed beads: Whimbeads.com. Ceramic spacers: The Mykonos. Lampworked glass discs: Kab's Creative Concepts.

Designer Kerry Bogert

GLITTERATI

○○○

MATERIALS

5" (12.7 cm) of dark annealed steel 19-gauge wire

4½" (11.4 cm) of dark annealed steel 28-gauge wire

3 Comet Argent Light AB 4mm Swarovski crystal bicones

1 pair gunmetal French ear wires

TOOLS

Flush cutters

Chain-nose pliers

Round-nose pliers

Ball-peen hammer

Bench block

FINISHED SIZE

2⅛" (5.4 cm)

1. Cut the 19-gauge wire in half. Cut the 28-gauge wire into three 1½" (3.8 cm) pieces.

2. Use round-nose pliers to form a simple oval loop using ½" of the end of one 19-gauge wire.

3. Use chain-nose pliers to spiral the wire slightly so that it resembles the top of an S shape.

4. Use round-nose pliers to form a small loop on the other end of the wire, twisting in the opposite direction of the first loop.

5. Use chain-nose pliers to spiral the wire so that it resembles the bottom of an S shape. Use the hammer to flatten the S shape.

6. Use round- and chain-nose pliers to make a tiny spiral on one end of one 28-gauge wire. Repeat twice for a total of three spirals. Use the ball end of the hammer to gently texture the spirals.

7. Use 1 spiral to string 1 bicone. Form a wrapped loop that attaches to the bottom of the S shape. Repeat with the other two spirals.

8. Attach 1 ear wire to the top of the S shape.

9. Repeat Steps 2 to 8 for the second earring.

RESOURCE: Ear wires: Artbeads.com.

Designer Leslie Rogalski

BLUE BY YOU

MATERIALS
4 blue 10mm ID aluminum jump rings

2 blue 8mm enamel rings

1 pair sterling silver ear wires

TOOLS
2 pairs of chain-nose pliers

FINISHED SIZE
1⅝" (4.1 cm)

1. Open all 4 jump rings.

2. Attach 2 jump rings to each enamel ring.

3. Attach each ear wire to 1 jump ring on each set.

Alternative: Use hammered sterling jump rings for an earthier look.

RESOURCES: Aluminum jump rings: The Ring Lord. Enamel rings: Michaels.

CHEERY O'S

MATERIALS
10" of sterling silver 18-gauge dead-soft wire

TOOLS
Flush cutters

Ring mandrel

Chain-nose pliers

File or wire smoother

Sharpie

FINISHED SIZE
1¾" (4.4 cm)

1. Use size 4 on the ring mandrel to form a wrapped loop on one end of 5" (12.7 cm) of wire.

2. Use the ball end of the ball-peen hammer to add texture to the loop.

3. Use the Sharpie and the other end of the wire to form an ear wire. Use the file to smooth the end of the ear wire.

4. Repeat Steps 1 to 3 for the second earring.

Alternative: Use blackened steel for a punk look!

ASIAN INFLUENCE

○○

MATERIALS

8" (20.3 cm) of sterling silver 16-gauge dead-soft wire

2 sterling silver 18-gauge 6mm jump rings

2 sterling silver 20-gauge 4mm jump rings

2 sterling silver 24-gauge 1" (2.5 cm) head pins

2 Crystal Silver Shade Swarovski crystal rondelles

1 pair sterling silver ear wires

TOOLS

Flush cutters

Ring mandrel

Chain-nose pliers

Ball-peen hammer

Bench block

Liver of sulfur (optional)

Disposable cup (optional)

Plastic spoon (optional)

FINISHED SIZE

1⅞" (4.8 cm)

1. Cut the wire in half.

2. Hold the center of 1 piece of wire against the ring mandrel at size 10 and bend both ends around the mandrel until they cross each other. Repeat entire step to form a second hoop.

3. Use the hammer and bench block to flatten both hoops. Repeat to flatten both 6mm jump rings and both 4mm jump rings.

4. Attach one 6mm jump ring around 1 hoop where the wires cross.

5. Use one 4mm jump ring to attach 1 ear wire to the 6mm jump ring.

6. Use 1 head pin to string 1 crystal. Form a wrapped loop that attaches to the 6mm jump ring.

7. Repeat Steps 4 to 6 for the second earring.

8. Use liver of sulfur to oxidize the earrings.

RESOURCE: Crystals: Michaels.

SWINGERS

MATERIALS
2" (5.1 cm) of sterling silver 20-gauge dead-soft wire

2" (5.1 cm) of sterling silver 24-gauge dead-soft wire

2 blue/yellow 12mm lampworked glass beads

2 blue quartz 7mm faceted rondelles

1 pair sterling silver ear wires

TOOLS
Flush cutters

Chain-nose pliers

Round-nose pliers

FINISHED SIZE
1½" (3.8 cm)

1. Cut the 20-gauge wire in half. Cut the 24-gauge wire in half and make 2 head pins.

2. Use 1 head pin to string 1 blue quartz rondelle. Form a wrapped loop.

3. Use one 20-gauge wire to form a simple loop. String 1 lampworked glass bead. Form a simple loop that attaches to the wrapped loop formed in Step 2.

4. Attach 1 ear wire to the other simple loop.

5. Repeat Steps 2 to 4 for the second earring.

RESOURCES: Lampworked glass beads: Grace Lampwork Beads and Jewelry Inc. Faceted blue quartz rondelles: House of Gems.

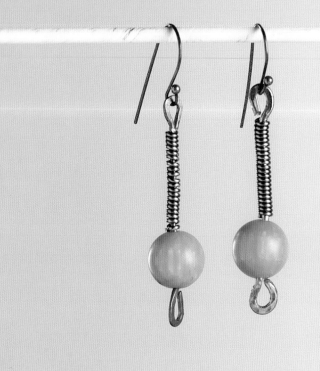

STICKBALL

MATERIALS

5" (12.7 cm) of copper 14-gauge wire

About 36" (91.4 cm) of purple 22-gauge ParaWire craft wire worked from the spool

2 matte green 12mm Lucite round beads

1 pair copper ear wires

TOOLS

Flush cutters

Heavy-duty cutters

Chain-nose pliers

Round-nose pliers

Ball-peen hammer

Bench block

FINISHED SIZE

2¼" (5.7 cm)

Note: Use heavy-duty cutters to cut your copper wire; this gauge can damage better cutters.

1. Cut the copper wire in half.

2. Use round-nose pliers to make a simple loop on one end of 1 copper wire.

3. String 1 bead. Use the other end of the wire to form 1 simple loop, slightly larger than and on the same plane as the previous loop.

4. Use the ball-peen hammer to texture the loops, carefully avoiding the long section of wire and the bead.

5. Push the round bead snug against the larger loop. Working from the spool of purple wire, coil tightly around the long part of the wire to fill the entire space between the round bead and the top loop. Push the wraps together with your fingernail as you work. End the coil on the same side of the wire as you started; trim the end with regular wire cutters.

6. Attach 1 ear wire to the top loop.

7. Repeat Steps 2 to 5 for the second earring.

RESOURCES: Copper wire: Caldron Crafts. Matte Lucite beads: The Beadin' Path. Purple wire: Paramount Wire Co.

Designer Leslie Rogalski

SIMPLIFY

◎

MATERIALS
4" (10.2 cm) of fine silver 20-gauge half-hard wire

TOOLS
Flush cutters

Butane torch

Ball-peen hammer

Bench block

File or wire smoother

Polishing cloth

Sharpie

FINISHED SIZE
⅝" (1.6 cm)

1. Cut the wire in half.

2. Use the torch to ball up one end of 1 wire and quench to cool.

3. Bend the wire over the Sharpie.

4. Hammer the curve of the earring to work-harden.

5. Trim to length and polish. Use a file to smooth the wire end.

6. Repeat Steps 2 to 5 for the second earring.

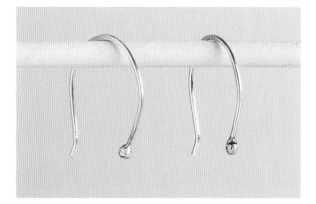

FREE WHEELIN'

◎

MATERIALS
5" (12.7 cm) of black 3mm chain

2 green/blue 20mm lampworked glass discs

1 pair sterling silver ear wires

TOOLS
Flush cutters

Chain-nose pliers

FINISHED SIZE
2" (5.1 cm)

1. Cut the chain in half.

2. Use 1 chain to string 1 disc. Attach 1 ear wire to both ends of chain.

3. Repeat Step 2 for the second earring.

RESOURCES: Lampworked glass disc beads: Blue Heeler Glass. Chain: Whimbeads.com.

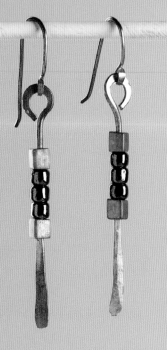

COPPER STICKS

○

MATERIALS

4" (10.2 cm) of copper 16-gauge wire

3" (8.9 cm) of copper 20-gauge wire

6 bronze size 6° seed beads

4 green 4mm cube seed beads

TOOLS

Flush cutters

Chain-nose pliers

Round-nose pliers

Ball-peen hammer

Bench block

File or wire smoother

Ruler

Sharpie

FINISHED SIZE

2⅛" (5.4 cm)

1. Cut the 16-gauge wire in half.

2. Hammer one end of 1 wire into a flat paddle ⅝" (1.6 cm) long.

3. Use the other end of the wire to string 1 cube, 3 seed beads, and 1 cube. Form a simple loop at the end, making sure the loop and the flat part of the paddle are on the same plane.

4. Hammer the simple loop flat. Use chain-nose pliers to reshape the loop as needed.

5. Cut the 20-gauge wire in half.

6. Hammer one end of 1 wire to flatten the end with the hammer. Use round-nose pliers to form a small loop on the flattened end of the wire. Before completing the loop, string the simple loop formed in Step 3. Complete the loop.

7. Bend the wire over the Sharpie, creating the ear wire. Use chain-nose pliers to grasp the tip of the ear wire and create a slight bend away from the earring. Use the file to smooth the end of the ear wire.

8. Repeat Steps 1 to 4, 6, and 7 for the second earring.

RESOURCES: Copper wire: Metalliferous. Bronze seed beads: Blue Santa Beads.

Designer Jane Dickerson

LEARNING CURVE

○○

MATERIALS

12" of sterling silver 20-gauge dead-soft wire

2 blue 12mm ceramic spacers

2 blue 18mm lampworked glass discs

1 pair sterling silver ear wires

TOOLS

Flush cutters

Chain-nose pliers

Round-nose pliers

FINISHED SIZE

1½" (3.8 cm)

1. Cut the wire in half.

2. Use round- and chain-nose pliers to create a spiral with four full rings of spiral.

3. To build the spiral frame, use chain-nose pliers to make a 90° bend in the wire near the end of the spiral. Make the bend a continuation of the spiral, not going in the opposite direction of it. Form a 90° bend about ⅜" (1 cm) from the previous bend. Form a third 90° bend ⅜" (1 cm) from the previous bend.

4. At what will be the top of the frame, use round-nose pliers to make a loop before continuing to bend the frame. Form a 90° bend about ⅜" (1 cm) from the previous bend. Form a 90° bend that curves around the first bend made.

5. Form a 90° bend about ¼" (0.6 cm) from and in the opposite direction of the previous bend so that it is perpendicular to the frame and opposite the loop.

6. String 1 ceramic spacer and 1 disc. Use round-nose pliers to grasp the end of the wire and spiral it in toward the disc.

7. Attach 1 ear wire to the top loop of the frame.

8. Repeat Steps 2 to 7 for the second earring.

RESOURCES: Ceramic beads: The Mykonos. Lampworked glass discs: Kab's Creative Concepts.

Designer Kerry Bogert

LET'S HOOK UP

◎◎

MATERIALS
4 copper 14-gauge 14mm jump rings

2 rubber 18mm OD O-rings

2 copper 5×12mm figure-eight connectors

1 pair copper ear wires

TOOLS
Chain-nose pliers

Round-nose pliers

FINISHED SIZE
2¼" (5.7 cm)

1. Use both pliers to open one end of 1 connector. Attach it to 1 copper ring. Close connector.

2. Use both pliers to open the other end of the same connector. Attach it to 1 rubber ring and 1 copper ring. Close connector.

3. Attach 1 ear wire to the copper ring used in Step 1.

4. Repeat Steps 1 to 4 for the second earring.

RESOURCES: Copper connectors, ear wires, and jump rings: Gems and Findings. Rubber O-rings: Local hardware store.

Designer: Leslie Rogalski

ENCIRCLED

◎

MATERIALS

10" (25.4 cm) of bronze 20-gauge craft wire

TOOLS

Flush cutters

Round-nose pliers

File or wire smoother

Sharpie

FINISHED SIZE

1¾" (4.4 cm)

1. Cut the wire in half.

2. Use round-nose pliers to make a loop at one end of 1 wire.

3. Holding the wire right next to the loop just made, use round-nose pliers to make another loop the same size as the previous loop.

4. Repeat Step 3 three times.

5. Bend the rest of the wire over the Sharpie to make the ear wire. Trim to desired length and use the file to smooth the end.

6. Repeat Steps 2 to 5 for the second earring.

Alternative: Dangle a bead from the bottom loop.

RESOURCE: ParaWire craft wire: Paramount Wire Co.

SQUARE OFF

⊚⊚
MATERIALS
5" (12.7 cm) of sterling silver 24-gauge wire

1½" (3.8 cm) of sterling silver 20-gauge wire

2 sterling silver 8mm square soldered jump rings

8 copper-plated 4mm daisy spacers

1 pair sterling silver ear wires

TOOLS
Flush cutters

Chain-nose pliers

Round-nose pliers

Liver of sulfur (optional)

Disposable cup (optional)

Plastic spoon (optional)

Polishing pad

FINISHED SIZE
1½" (3.8 cm)

1. Create a coil by wrapping the 24-gauge wire neatly around the 20-gauge wire until you have a little more than ½" (1.3 cm). Slip the coil off of the 20-gauge wire. Trim the excess 24-gauge wire, leaving a neat, tight coil.

2. Use liver of sulfur to oxidize the coil. Rinse and dry. Use the polishing pad to remove any excess patina and polish the wire.

3. Cut the coiled wire into two ¼" (0.6 cm) pieces. Cut the 20-gauge wire in half.

4. Use round-nose pliers and one 20-gauge wire to form a simple loop that attaches to 1 jump ring. Use the wire to string 2 copper spacers, 1 coil, and 2 copper spacers. Form a simple loop that attaches to 1 ear wire.

5. Repeat Step 4 for the second earring.

RESOURCES: Heishi: TierraCast. Ear wires: You and Me Findings. Square closed rings, liver of sulfur, and Pro polishing pad: Rio Grande. Wire: T.B. Hagstoz.

Designer: Jane Dickerson

GOLDEN RINGS

○

MATERIALS

5" (12.7 cm) of gold-filled 26-gauge half-hard wire

2 red 7mm clay beads

1 pair gold-filled ear wires

TOOLS

Flush cutters

Large step mandrel

Chain-nose pliers

Round-nose pliers

Hammer

Bench block

FINISHED SIZE

1⅛" (2.9 cm)

1. Make 2 split rings by coiling the wire around the largest step on the mandrel, snip the rings so you leave a double coil on half of each jump ring.

2. Hammer only the single half of each split ring.

3. Use 1 split ring to string 1 bead.

4. Use round-nose pliers to form a loop on both wire ends.

5. Attach 1 ear wire to both loops.

6. Repeat Steps 3 to 5 for the second earring.

Alternative: Use 10mm round Swarovski pearls to create a classic.

RESOURCE: Clay beads: Embroidered Soul.

RIBBONS

○○

MATERIALS
36" (91.4 cm) of sterling silver 18-gauge dead-soft wire

1 pair sterling silver butterfly earring backs

TOOLS
Flush cutters

Round-nose pliers

Ball-peen hammer

Awl

Bench block

File or wire smoother

FINISHED SIZE
⅞" (2.2 cm)

1. Cut the wire in half.

2. Use the hammer to flatten all but the last 1" (2.5 cm) of wire. The unflattened end of the wire will become the earring post. Use the file to smooth the end of the post.

3. Use round-nose pliers to make a small loop on the flat end of the wire, then transfer the loop to the awl. Use the awl as a mandrel and wrap the entire length of flattened wire messily around it.

4. When you reach the 1" (2.5 cm) of unhammered wire, bend it out to the back of the earring to form the post.

5. Repeat Steps 2 to 4 for the second earring.

Alternative: Oxidize with liver of sulfur and polish the high spots.

THIS WAY + THAT

◎

MATERIALS

1½" (3.8 cm) of sterling silver 12-gauge dead-soft wire

1 pair sterling silver ear wires

TOOLS

Heavy-duty wire cutters

Hammer

Awl

Bench block

Liver of sulfur (optional)

Disposable cup (optional)

Plastic spoon (optional)

Metal file

FINISHED SIZE

1¼" (3.2 cm)

1. Cut the wire in half.

2. Hammer one half of 1 wire flat, splaying the end.

3. Turn the wire around, hold the piece so the flattened side is perpendicular to the block and hammer the other half.

4. Use the ball end of the hammer to texture both sides of both ends.

5. Use the awl and hammer to punch a hole in one end. Attach 1 ear wire to the hole.

6. Repeat Steps 2 to 5 for the second earring.

7. Use liver of sulfur to oxidize earrings.

Alternative: Tumble for a high polish instead of oxidizing.

VINTAGE

MATERIALS
6" (15.2 cm) of Vintage Bronze 20-gauge craft wire

2 antique 15mm shank buttons

TOOLS
Flush cutters

Round-nose pliers

File or wire smoother

Sharpie

FINISHED SIZE
1⅛" (2.9 cm)

1. Cut the wire in half.

2. Push one end of 1 wire just a bit through the shank, then wrap the wire once completely around the shank.

3. Bend the wire around a Sharpie to make an ear wire. Use the file to smooth the end.

4. Use round-nose pliers to make a small bend at the end of the ear wire.

5. Repeat Steps 2 to 4 for the second earring.

RESOURCES: Antique buttons: Check your local antique store. ParaWire craft wire: Paramount Wire Co.

STEEL STARBURSTS

○○○

MATERIALS
14" (35.6 cm) of annealed steel 19-gauge wire

10" (25.4 cm) of annealed steel 28-gauge wire

24 zinc size 8° seed beads

1 pair gunmetal ear wires

TOOLS
Flush cutters

Chain-nose pliers

Round-nose pliers

Ball-peen hammer

Bench block

FINISHED SIZE
1⅞" (4.8 cm)

1. Cut the 19-gauge wire into four 2" (5.1 cm) pieces and two 3" (7.6 cm) pieces.

2. Use round- and chain-nose pliers to spiral one end of one 2" (5.1 cm) wire. String 6 seed beads and spiral the other end of the wire in the opposite direction of the first spiral. Texture the spirals with the ball end of the hammer, avoiding the beads. Repeat entire step to make a second beaded, spiraled piece.

3. Spiral ¾" (1.9 cm) of one end of one 3" wire. Repeat on the other end of the wire in the opposite direction. Texture the spirals with the hammer.

4. Position the 3 spiraled wires with the unbeaded, longer wire in the middle. Separate the beads into 2 sets of 3 on each wire, with a space in the middle. Cut the 28-gauge wire in half and use one to wrap the 3 spiraled pieces together with a tight coil, keeping the beads separated so the coil is around empty wire in the middle of the wires. Trim wires on the back side of the earring.

5. Bend the beaded wires into "C" shapes to space them evenly into a starburst shape.

6. Repeat Steps 2 to 5 for the second earring.

RESOURCES: Zinc seed beads: Jane's Fibers and Beads. Ear wires: Artbeads.com.

Designer: Leslie Rogalski

STACKED

◎

MATERIALS
8" (20.3 cm) of sterling silver 20-gauge dead-soft wire

6 assorted 10mm lampworked glass rondelles

2 orange and white 16mm lampworked glass discs

1 pair sterling silver ear wires

TOOLS
Flush cutters

Chain-nose pliers

Round-nose pliers

FINISHED SIZE
1⅞" (4.8 cm)

1. Cut the wire into two 1½" (3.8 cm) pieces and two 2½" (6.4 cm) pieces.

2. Use round-nose pliers to form a small simple loop at the end of 1 short piece of wire. String 1 rondelle and form a wrapped loop.

3. Use round-nose pliers to form a small simple loop on one end of 1 long piece of wire. Attach the simple loop to the wrapped loop. String 1 rondelle, 1 disc, and 1 rondelle; form a wrapped loop.

4. Attach 1 ear wire to the wrapped loop.

5. Repeat Steps 2 to 4 for the second earring.

RESOURCES: Lampworked glass rondelles: Jewels by Shari. Lampworked glass discs: Blue Heeler Glass.

CASCADES

○○

MATERIALS

7" (17.8 cm) of sterling silver 24-gauge half-hard wire

6 pale blue 10×14mm metal flower bead caps

1 pair sterling silver ear wires

TOOLS

Flush cutters

Chain-nose pliers

Round-nose pliers

FINISHED SIZE

2⅜" (6 cm)

1. Cut the wire into four 1¼" (3.2 cm) pieces and two 1" (2.5 cm) pieces.

2. Use one 1¼" (3.2 cm) wire to form a simple loop. String 1 bead cap and form a simple loop.

3. Use one 1¼" (3.2 cm) wire to form a simple loop that attaches to the previous simple loop. String 1 bead cap and form a simple loop.

4. Use one 1" (2.5 cm) wire to form a simple loop that attaches to the previous simple loop. String 1 bead cap and form a wrapped loop that attaches to 1 ear wire.

5. Repeat Steps 2 to 4 for the second earring.

RESOURCE: Metal flower beads: Black Sheep Beads.

WATER DROPS

◎

MATERIALS
8" (20.3 cm) of sterling silver 20-gauge half-hard wire
2 borosilicate glass 10mm rondelles

TOOLS
Flush cutters
Ring mandrel
Chain-nose pliers
Round-nose pliers
File or wire smoother
Ruler
Sharpie

FINISHED SIZE
1½" (3.8 cm)

1. Cut the wire in half.

2. Use size 0 on the ring mandrel to begin a wrapped loop 2" (5.1 cm) from one end of 1 wire. Before you wrap it, hammer the loop lightly to flatten and string the bead. Wrap the loop.

3. Bend the other end of the wire around a Sharpie to make the ear wire. Use the file to smooth the end.

4. Repeat Steps 2 and 3 for the second earring.

Alternative: Use three or four 4mm cube seed beads for whimsy!

RESOURCE: Glass rondelles: Unicorne Beads.

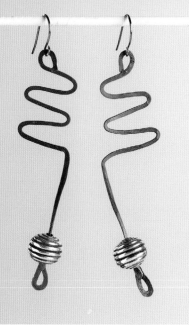

WINDING ROADS

⊙⊙

MATERIALS

14" (35.6 cm) of annealed steel 19-gauge wire

2 Bali silver 12×10mm large-hole round beads

1 pair gunmetal French ear wires

TOOLS

Flush cutters

Chain-nose pliers

Round-nose pliers

Ball-peen hammer

Bench block

Ruler

FINISHED SIZE

3½" (8.9 cm)

Note: Try to bend both wire shapes together at the same time to make them as similar as possible. If you find this challenging, create one wire shape at a time and match them side by side before hammering, allowing for adjustment.

1. Cut wire in half.

2. Use round-nose pliers to make an oval loop on one end of the wire, slightly overlapping the wire.

3. Use the edge of the metal ruler to help guide the wire curves and create acute angles, by bending the wire back and forth over the ruler's edge with your fingers into 2 to 3 zigzags of equal size. Keep the zigzags parallel and at a right angle to the loop. Bend the remaining wire end at a right angle to the last zigzag. Adjust the zigzags and wire with your fingers.

4. String 1 silver bead.

5. Use round-nose pliers to make an oval loop at the end of the wire, slightly overlapping the wire.

6. Carefully hammer the first loop and zigzag with the flat side of the hammer. The wire should appear to meld into itself where the wire overlaps. Push the silver bead up out of the way and hammer the remaining wire and loop. Slide the bead back down.

7. Attach 1 ear wire to the top loop.

8. Repeat Steps 2 to 7 for the second earring.

RESOURCES: Bali silver bead: Singaraja Imports. Ear wires: Artbeads.com.

Designer: Leslie Rogalski

LANTERNS

○ ○ ○

MATERIALS

8" (20.3 cm) of copper 18-gauge wire

10" (25.4 cm) of purple 20-gauge craft wire

8 matte blue size 6° seed beads

2 blue 12×4mm Lucite or resin saucers

1 pair copper ear wires

TOOLS

Flush cutters

¾" (1.9 cm) diameter dowel or mandrel

Chain-nose pliers

Round-nose pliers

Flat-nose pliers

Ball-peen hammer

Bench block

FINISHED SIZE

1⅞" (4.8 cm)

1. Cut the copper wire in half. Cut the purple wire in half.

2. Use round nose-pliers to hold the middle of 1 piece of copper wire; bend the wire over the jaw so the ends meet, forming a loop.

3. Keep the wire in the round-nose pliers and transfer the pliers to your non-dominant hand. Use flat-nose pliers to pinch the wire beneath the round nose, bringing the loop closed; the wire ends should be somewhat adjacent.

4. Reposition the flat-nose pliers to hold the wire loop flat. Split the two end wires and use your fingers to bend them around the dowel rod until they overlap and the ends point in opposite directions.

5. Remove the dowel and use chain-nose pliers to hold the crossed wires at the bottom of the circle. Use any pliers or your fingers to bend the wire ends down, at right angles to the circle and parallel to each other.

6. Use round-nose pliers to form a small single loop spiral at the end of each wire, curling up/outward.

7. Use the end of 1 purple wire to make 3 coiled wraps connecting the two bottom spirals, making sure the copper wires remain side by side and don't overlap. End the third coil at the back of the earring.

8. Use chain-nose pliers to bend the long end of the purple wire just above the coil, so it runs straight up through the center of the large circle space. Use the purple wire to string 2 seed beads, 1 saucer, and 2 seed beads.

9. Use chain-nose pliers to hold the purple wire centered between the copper wires of the top loop; use fingers to coil the purple wire three times around the "throat" of the loop. Complete the third coil in the back of the earring. Trim purple wires ends at the back of the earring. Use chain-nose pliers to secure the purple coils.

10. Attach 1 ear wire to the top loop.

11. Repeat Steps 2 to 11 for the second earring.

RESOURCES: Lucite saucers: Cherry Tree Beads. ParaWire craft wire: Paramount Wire Co.

Designer: Leslie Rogalski

DOUBLE COIL POSTS

○ ◯

MATERIALS
14" (35.6 cm) of copper 20-gauge wire

1 pair nylon butterfly earring backs

TOOLS
Flush cutters

Round-nose pliers

Flat-nose pliers

File or wire smoother

Ruler

FINISHED SIZE
⅞" (2.2 cm)

1. Cut the wire in half.
2. Use flat-nose pliers to make a 90° bend ⅜" (1 cm) from one end of 1 wire.
3. Use the tip of the round-nose pliers to hold the wire at the bend so that the short end is parallel with the nose of the pliers. Make a tiny loop.
4. Use flat-nose pliers to continue to spiral around the loop until 2" (5.1 cm) of wire remains.
5. Use the remaining wire to make another spiral, going in the opposite direction and stopping just before meeting the first spiral.
6. Repeat Steps 2 to 5 for the second earring. Attach 1 ear stopper to each post. Use the file to smooth the ends of the posts.

Alternative: Add a bead dangle to the bottom spiral for a little swing.

RESOURCE: Butterfly earring backs: Artbeads.com.

OVOIDS

◎

MATERIALS

8" (20.3 cm) of sterling silver 20-gauge dead-soft wire

2 green 10×30mm enamel metal ovals

2 teal 12mm lampworked glass rondelles

1 pair sterling silver ear wires

TOOLS

Flush cutters

Round-nose pliers

FINISHED SIZE

2¼" (5.7 cm)

1. Cut the wire in half.
2. Use round-nose pliers and 1 wire to form a simple loop that attaches to 1 metal oval. String 1 lampworked glass rondelle.
3. Form a wrapped loop atop the bead but do not cut the tail. Continue spiraling the tail snugly around the top of the bead to form a bead cap.
4. Attach 1 ear wire to the wrapped loop.
5. Repeat Steps 2 to 4 for the second earring.

RESOURCES: Enamel rings: Stone Mountain. Lampworked glass beads: Joanne Zekowski.

CLIMBING VINES

◎
MATERIALS
9" (22.9 cm) of sterling silver 20-gauge
  half-hard square wire

3" (7.6 cm) of sterling silver 20-gauge
  dead-soft square wire

2 lampworked glass 12mm beads

TOOLS
Flush cutters

Large stepped mandrel

Chain-nose pliers

Round-nose pliers

File or wire smoother

Ruler

Sharpie

FINISHED SIZE
2¼" (5.7 cm)

1. Cut the dead-soft wire in half.

2. Use round-nose pliers to form a simple loop at one end of 1 wire. String 1 bead and form a wrapped loop. Repeat entire step with the other wire. Set aside.

3. Cut the half-hard wire in half.

4. Make a mark ¾" (1.9 cm) from one end of the wire and bend it at that point over the second largest step on the stepped mandrel.

5. Make a mark 1½" (3.8 cm) from the first bend and bend the wire over the second smallest step on the stepped mandrel.

6. Hang 1 bead charm on the second bend and wrap the end of the wire up the ear wire like a vine, starting about 1" (2.5 cm) from the second bend.

7. Trim after 2 wraps. Use chain-nose pliers to pinch the end snugly against the ear wire.

8. Use the file to smooth the end of the ear wire.

9. Repeat Steps 4 to 8 for the second earring.

RESOURCE: Lampwork beads: Natalia Designs

COPPER SPARKS

MATERIALS

8" (20.3 cm) of copper 16-gauge wire

About 36" (91.4 cm) of copper 28-gauge wire worked
    from the spool

36 translucent copper 3×9mm top-drilled pressed-glass
    daggers

1 pair copper ear wires

TOOLS

Flush cutters

¾" (1.9 cm) diameter wooden dowel or mandrel

Round-nose pliers

Flat-nose pliers

FINISHED SIZE

2¼" (5.7 cm)

1. Cut the 16-gauge wire in half.

2. Use the dowel and flat-nose pliers to form a simple
   loop on one end of 1 piece of wire.

3. Use round-nose pliers to hold the wire 1" (2.5 cm)

above the loop. Bend the wire 180° over the nose of the
pliers to form a loop and pinch the two wires together.
Make sure the pinched wires and the loop are on the
same plane.

4. Do not cut the 28-gauge wire from the spool. Use the
   28-gauge wire to string 18 daggers.

5. Use the 28-gauge wire to make one complete wrap
   around the 16-gauge stem. Move 6 to 8 of the daggers
   to the stem, enough to wrap daggers evenly in one
   complete circle around the stem. Move the remaining
   daggers to the stem and continue to wrap the wire
   around it. The cluster of daggers should spike out
   around the stem.

6. Continue wrapping tightly around the stem all the way
   up to the top loop, leaving the loop exposed. Trim wire
   end at the back of the earring. Trim any excess wire
   beneath the daggers where the wrapping began.

7. Attach 1 ear wire to the top loop.

8. Repeat Steps 2 to 7 for the second earring.

RESOURCES: Copper wire: Caldron Crafts. Daggers: The
Blushing Bead.

Designer: Leslie Rogalski

PLANETS

MATERIALS

2 sterling silver 22-gauge 1½" (3.8 cm) head pins

2 sterling silver 17mm hammered cut-out rings

2 purple/green 11mm borosilicate glass round beads

1 pair sterling silver ear wires

TOOLS

Flush cutters

Chain-nose pliers

Round-nose pliers

FINISHED SIZE

1¾" (4.4 cm)

1. Use 1 head pin to string 1 glass round. Form a wrapped loop that attaches to 1 hammered ring.

2. Attach 1 ear wire to the opposite side of the hammered ring.

3. Repeat Steps 1 and 2 for the second earring.

Alternative: Dangle 5 Swarovski crystals in place of the glass round.

RESOURCES: Hammered cut-out rings: Fusionbeads.com. Borosilicate beads: Unicorne Beads.

SEAWATER

◎

MATERIALS
6¼" (3.8 cm) of sterling silver 20-gauge half-hard wire

6 blue quartz 8mm faceted rondelles

TOOLS
Flush cutters

Chain-nose pliers

Round-nose pliers

Ball-peen hammer

Bench block

File or wire smoother

Ruler

FINISHED SIZE
1¼" (3.2 cm)

1. Cut the wire in half.
2. Use the hammer to splay one end of 3⅛" (7.9 cm) of wire.
3. String 3 rondelles.
4. Mark 1¼" (3.2 cm) from the other end of the wire. Mark again 1½" (3.8 cm) from the first mark.
5. Use chain-nose pliers to make a 90° bend at the first mark and another 90° bend at the second mark.
6. Use round-nose pliers to make a small curve at the end of the ear wire. Use the file to smooth the end.
7. Repeat Steps 2 to 6 for second earring.

Alternative: Use 8mm pearls for sophistication.

RESOURCE: Blue quartz beads: Lima Beads.

PEARL NESTS

◎◎◎

MATERIALS

4" (10.2 cm) of sterling silver 20-gauge dead-soft wire

2 blue/green 14×8mm borosilicate glass rondelles

18 pale green 5–7mm center-drilled keishi pearls

18 sterling silver 22-gauge ¾" (1.9 cm) head pins

4 silver 5mm daisy spacers

1 pair sterling silver ear wires

TOOLS

Flush cutters

Round-nose pliers

FINISHED SIZE

1⅜" (3.5 cm)

1. Use 1 head pin to string 1 keishi pearl; form a small wrapped loop. Repeat seventeen times for a total of 18 dangles.

2. Cut the wire in half. Make one end of each half into an eye pin or head pin.

3. Use 1 eye pin/head pin to string 1 daisy spacer, 1 glass rondelle, 9 dangles, and 1 daisy spacer. Form a wrapped loop that attaches to 1 ear wire.

4. Repeat Step 3 for the second earring.

Alternative: Use a 15mm round pearl for a very elegant look.

RESOURCES: Borosilicate glass beads: Pumpkin Hill Beads. Keishi pearls: Abeadstore.com.

CARNELIAN COILS

○ ○

MATERIALS
12" (30.5 cm) of sterling silver 20-gauge half-hard wire

4 carnelian 5×3mm faceted rondelles

1 pair sterling silver ear wires

TOOLS
Flush cutters

Large step mandrel

Chain-nose pliers

Round-nose pliers

FINISHED SIZE
2½" (6.4 cm)

1. Cut the wire in half.
2. Bend 1 wire in half over the largest step on the mandrel.
3. Use 1 end of the wire to string 1 carnelian rondelle. Use round-nose pliers to form a tiny loop on the wire end. Repeat entire step for the other end of wire.
4. Wrap 1 end of the wire around the middle step on the mandrel and then gently pull to stretch out the coils. Repeat with the other wire end.
5. Attach 1 ear wire to the middle of the wire.
6. Repeat Steps 2 to 5 for the second earring.

Alternative: Use faceted turquoise beads for an earthy look.

RESOURCE: Carnelian beads: Fire Mountain Gems and Beads.

ANCIENT GLASS ORBS

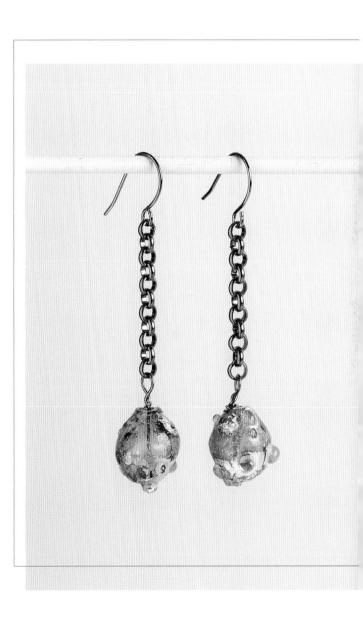

MATERIALS

2" (5.1 cm) of gunmetal 2mm rolo chain

2 gray 12mm Venetian hollow glass orb beads

2 gunmetal 2" (5.1 cm) head pins

1 pair gunmetal ear wires

TOOLS

Flush cutters

Chain-nose pliers

Round-nose pliers

FINISHED SIZE

2⅜" (6 cm)

1. Cut the chain in half.

2. Use 1 head pin to string 1 glass bead. Form a wrapped loop that attaches to one end of 1 chain.

3. Attach 1 ear wire to the other end of the chain.

4. Repeat Steps 2 and 3 for the second earring.

Alternative: 14mm round white pearls will show off the gunmetal chain.

RESOURCES: Glass beads: Lady from Venice. Gunmetal rolo chain: Whimbeads.com. Gunmetal ear wires: Artbeads.com.

STEEL MAGNOLIAS

◯◯◯

MATERIALS

20" (50.8 cm) of annealed steel 19-gauge wire

16" (61 cm) of annealed steel 28-gauge wire

2 matte yellow 20mm Lucite flowers with center-drilled hole

2 Crystal Golden Shadow 2mm Swarovski crystal rounds

1 pair gunmetal ear wires

TOOLS

Flush cutters

¾" (1.9 cm) diameter wood dowel or mandrel

Chain-nose pliers

Round-nose pliers

Ball-peen hammer

Bench block

FINISHED SIZE

2⅜" (6 cm)

1. Cut the 19-gauge wire in half. Cut the 28-gauge wire into four 2" (5.1 cm) pieces and two 4" (10.2 cm) pieces.

2. Bottom left loop. Use round-nose pliers to hold one 19-gauge wire ½" (1.3 cm) in from one end. Bend the short end toward you around the pliers' nose in a simple oval loop so it slightly overlaps the long wire.

3. Bottom center loop. Reposition the round-nose pliers to hold the long end of the wire at the overlap point. Use fingers to make a gentle curve toward you with the long wire. The two loops formed so far should point at right angles to each other.

4. Bottom right loop. Reposition the round-nose pliers ½" (1.3 cm) down the long wire from the overlap point. Use fingers to curve the long wire up around the round-nose pliers to form another simple oval loop, crossing the overlap point. The wire end should now point in the opposite direction from your first oval loop. Reposition the round-nose pliers to make a third loop, bending the long wire around the nose of the pliers to form the loop, and gently curving it up over the crossover point.

5. Top loop and large central shape. Use round-nose pliers to hold the long wire 1½" (3.8 cm) above the crossover of the three bottom loops. Bend the wire around the nose of the pliers to form a small loop.

6. Hold the top loop just formed flat in the chain-nose pliers. Center a dowel between the two lengths of wire and use fingers to bend the wires around the dowel, forming a marquis shape. The loose end of wire should overlap the bottom three loops at the crossover point. Use fingers and pliers to carefully make the shape symmetrical, reinserting the dowel as needed.

7. Repeat Steps 2 to 6 for the second earring, using the first earring as a template. Hammer both earring shapes to flatten. The overlap sections should appear to meld into each other.

8. Use one 2" (5.1 cm) wire to bind the bottom right loop to the bottom curve of the larger shape: make small, tight coils so the wires meet but do not overlap. Repeat to bind the bottom left loop to the bottom curve of the larger shape.

9. Use one 4" (10.2 cm) wire to string 1 crystal to the center of the wire. Use chain-nose pliers to pinch the two wires together, so they are centered under the crystal. Use both ends of the wire to string 1 Lucite flower, front to back.

10. String both wires through the middle of all crossover points in the earring shape. Separate the wires and make neat wraps around the crossover points of the side loops. Trim.

11. Attach 1 ear wire to the top loop.

12. Repeat Steps 8 to 10 for the second earring.

RESOURCES: Ear wires: Artbeads.com. Vintage German Lucite matte flower: The Beadin' Path.

Designer: Leslie Rogalski

RESOURCES

A.F. Silver Design LLC
51 Dante Ave.
Hicksville, NY 11801
(516) 731-0255
afsilverdesign.com

Abeadstore.com
(800) 532-8480
abeadstore.com

Anil Kumar / Nigam
PO Box 3471
Fremont, CA 94539

Artbeads.com
(866) 715-2323
artbeads.com

Bead Paradise II
29 West College St.
Oberlin, OH 44074
(440) 775-2233
beadparadise.com

The Beadin' Path
15 Main St.
Freeport, ME 04032
(877) 92-BEADS
beadinpath.com

Beads of Passion
beadsofpassion.etsy.com

Black Sheep Beads
blacksheepbeads.etsy.com

Blue Santa Beads
18 North Pennell Rd.
Media, PA 19063
(610) 892-2740
bluesanta-beads.com

Blue Heeler Glass
bluhealer.etsy.com

The Blushing Bead
(800) 900-3777
theblushingbead.com

Caldron Crafts
6611 Rte. 40 W.
Catonsville, MD 21228
(410) 744-2155
caldroncrafts.com

Cherry Tree Beads
(828) 505-2328
cherrytreebeads.com

Columbian Crafts
7655 Braeswood #51
Houston, TX 77071
(713) 995-8469
colombiancraftconnection.com

Eclectica
18900 W. Bluemound Rd.
Brookfield, WI 53045
(262) 641-0910
eclecticabeads.com

Embroidered Soul
(740) 965-4851
embroideredsoul.com

Fire Mountain Gems and Beads
One Fire Mountain Wy.
Grants Pass, OR 97526-2373
(800) 355-2137
firemountaingems.com

Fusion Beads
(888) 781-3559
fusionbeads.com

Gems and Findings
gemsandfindings.com

Grace Lampwork Beads and Jewelry Inc.
PO Box 360468
Milpitas, CA 95036
(408) 526-9700
gracebeads.com

Hands of the Hills
3016 78th Ave. SE
Mercer Island, WA 98040
(206) 232-4588
hohbead.com

Hanson Stone
(503) 206-6922
hanson-stone.com

Holy and Pure Gemstones
254-15 Northern Blvd.
Little Neck, NY 11362
(718) 225-6850
holygemstone.com

House of Gems
(213) 624-6280
houseofgems.com

Jane's Fibers and Beads
5415 East Andrew Johnson Hwy.
PO Box 110
Afton, TN 37616
(888) 497-2665
janesfibersandbeads.com

Jewelry Supply
(916) 780-9610
jewelrysupply.com

Jewels by Shari
jewelsbyshari.etsy.com

Joan Miller Porcelain Beads
joanmiller.com

Joanne Zekowski
rzekowski@mindspring.com

Jay Chantell
Jocelyn and Alex Pappadakis
jaychantell.com

Kab's Creative Concepts
Kerry Bogert
5799 Coppersmith Tr.
Ontario, NY 14519
(585) 944-0141
kabsconcepts.com

Lady from Venice
theladyfromvenice.com

Lima Beads
(888) 211-7919
limabeads.com

Metalliferous
34 W. 46th St.
New York, NY 10036
(212) 944-0909
metalliferous.com

Michaels Stores
michaels.com

Multi Creations Inc.
(732) 607-6422
multicreationsnj.com

My Elements by Yvonne
410 Butter Rd.
York, PA 17404
(717) 292-6678
myelementsbyyvonne.com

The Mykonos
245 Main St.
Hyannis, MA 02601
(888) MYKONOS
mykonosbeads.com

Natalia Designs
nataliadesigns.com

Natural Touch Beads
PO Box 2713
Petaluma, CA 94953
(707) 781-0808
naturaltouchbeads.com

Paramount Wire Co.
2-8 Central Ave.
East Orange, NJ 07018
(973) 672-0500
parawire.com

Pumpkin Hill Beads
(860) 350-3167
pumpkinhillbeads.com

The Ring Lord
290C RR6
Saskatoon SK
Canada S7K 3J9
(306) 374-1335
theringlord.com

Rio Grande
7500 Bluewater Rd. NW
Albuquerque, NM 87121-1962
(800) 545-6566
riogrande.com

Riverstone Bead Company
6131 Hemlock Ave.
Miller Beach, IN 46403
(219) 939-2050
riverstonebead.com

Singaraja Imports
94 Main St.
PO Box 4624
Vineyard Haven, MA 02568
(800) 865-8856
singarajaimports.com

Splendid Loon Studio
726 Tuckertown Rd.
Wakefield, RI 02879
(401) 789-7879
slsstudio.com

Stone Mountain
Ben Eagle
(719) 728-3202

Sunyno
sunyno.etsy.com

T.B. Hagstoz
709 Sanson St.
Philadelphia, PA 19106
(800) 922-1006
hagstoz.com

TierraCast (wholesale only)
3177 Guerneville Rd.
Santa Rosa, CA 95401
(800) 222-9939
tierracast.com

Unicorne Beads
404 Evelyn Place, Ste. D.
Placentia, CA 92870
(800) 833-2095
unicornebeads.com

Out On A Whim
121 E. Cotati Ave.
Cotati, CA 94931
(800) 232-3111
whimbeads.com

Wraps, Stones, and Things LLC
888 Brannan St., Ste. 602
San Francisco, CA 94103
(415) 863-4953
beadsnclasps.com

You and Me Findings
youandmefindings.net

CONTRIBUTORS

KERRY BOGERT

Kerry Bogert is the lampwork glass artist and wire jewelry designer behind Kab's Creative Concepts. She has been working with glass and wire for more than five years and is currently working with Interweave on her first book, due in the Spring 2010. To find out more about her work, visit kabsconcepts.com or contact her at kerry@kabsconcepts.com.

DENISE PECK

Denise Peck is the editor in chief of *Step by Step Wire Jewelry* magazine and author of *Wire Style*. A lifelong lover of jewelry, Denise went to jewelry-making school in New York City in 1999 to get her bench jeweler's certificate and joined *Lapidary Journal* in 2004. Her first instructional DVD on Viking knit technique was released in 2008 for the Bead Fest Video Workshops series.

JANE DICKERSON

Jane Dickerson is managing editor of *Step by Step Beads*, editor of *Creative Jewelry*, contributing editor to *Step by Step Wire Jewelry*, and project manager for the first series of Bead Fest educational jewelry-making DVDs and videos, Bead Fest Video Workshops. Her work has appeared in *Step by Step Beads*, *Creative Jewelry*, *Jewelry Gifts for the Holiday*, and *Easy Wire*.

LESLIE ROGALSKI

Leslie Rogalski is editor in chief of *Step by Step Beads* and *Creative Jewelry* and a contributing editor to *Step by Step Wire Jewelry*. A frequent presenter on the PBS TV show *Beads, Baubles & Jewels*, she has been an artist and writer (among other things) all her life.

INDEX

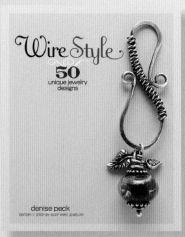

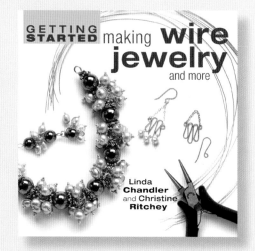